Foreword by Steve Gallagher

MW01077311

THE Radical JESUS

Glenn Meldrum

THE Radical JESUS

Glenn Meldrum

For books and other teaching resources please contact:

Pure Life Ministries
14 School Street
Dry Ridge, KY 41035
(888) PURELIFE - to order
www.purelifeministries.org

The Radical Jesus
Copyright © 2021 by Pure Life Ministries.

ISBN/EAN 978-0-578-86208-8

Contents

Foreword

One of the great dangers of our day is spiritual apathy. We live in a time when everything around us is conspiring to lull believers to sleep spiritually. Oh, how effortless it is to be careless about the things of God and excited about the things of the world. How natural it is to be lazy about seeking the Lord and wide awake for the world's various forms of entertainment.

The great need of the hour is for men of God who understand what it means to spend long hours in His Word and in His presence. Such men possess the spiritual sensitivity to bring a fresh word from the Lord for His people.

How tragic then that many of the popular preachers of our time are presenting a "dumbed down" form of the Gospel that is keeping Christians in a dangerous stupor. If these charlatans actually spent time on their faces before God, they wouldn't portray Him as a mere step or two above mankind; they wouldn't offer their audiences such a milquetoast version of Jesus Christ.

Thankfully, God has always been faithful to raise up watchmen to sound the alarm when His people have drifted into a spirit of slumber. Glenn Meldrum is one such man and the message he brings forth in this book is that Jesus is so glorious, so awe inspiring, so altogether "Other," that the only human word which can begin to adequately describe Him is "radical." And this is the very thing believers need to see today: Jesus Christ as He actually is in all His glory.

Jesus predicted that the last days would be a time when Christians would be dull of heart. He said *"all"* would become drowsy and fall asleep (Matthew 25:5). And it is certainly true that every one of us has drifted into such apathy at times. The difference between the sincere and insincere Christian is how they respond when the watchman sounds the alarm (Matthew 25:6-10).

I implore you not to be like those unprepared virgins or the spiritual sluggard who, when he *"hears the alarm, his response is, 'A little sleep, a little slumber, a little folding of the hands to rest'"* (Proverbs 24:33).

If you find yourself drifting into the soul-numbing lethargy of our day, this book is for you. God has put into your hands a flashing red light, a wailing siren. It is meant to wake you up and keep you awake. Read this book on your knees. Pay strict attention to its warnings. Open your heart to the Lord. If you will treat the message of this book with the kind of earnestness it deserves, you very well may find a new passion rising up within you to be like "The Radical Jesus" who is presented in its pages.

—Steve Gallagher

Introduction

The common conception that revolves around authors of nonfiction books is that they are experts on the subject in which they are writing. At times this may be true. Of course, there are also many authors who think they know far more than they really do. We want authors, when writing about the True and Living God, to be spiritually discerning, intellectually accurate and relationally faithful. We need them to present the truth in as pure a form as possible, for to err in this subject can hold dire consequences.

As mortals, we have an inherent problem when writing about the Lord God: He is infinitely bigger than we are. God is ineffable, which signifies that human words are incapable of properly describing Him. He is incomprehensible, which tells us He is impossible to understand because He is beyond human intellect. The Lord is inscrutable, which denotes that we are unable to fully investigate Him since He is an infinite mystery. He is inexplicable, meaning humans do not have the wherewithal to adequately explain or account for Him. All these dimensions of God indicate that the Almighty is infinitely beyond the understanding of finite men and angels. There are mysteries about Jesus that we will never fully understand even in the world to come and honest Christians readily admit how ignorant they are about Him.

So let me confess from the outset that I am not an expert on The Radical Jesus. What I am sharing with you in this book is a journey I am on, a quest to know Jesus in a deeper, more life-changing way. I do not claim to know much nor do I present anything beyond what the sacred Scriptures clearly teach about this wonderful Jesus. All I can say is that I have hungered to know Christ: not a manmade Jesus fashioned with the finite hands of fallen people or manipulated by a lukewarm church culture. No! I want to know the majestic Jesus, the Creator God who died upon the Cross to rescue mankind. I want to know the One who calls us *"together with all the saints, to grasp how wide and long and high and deep is the love of Christ, and to know this love that surpasses knowledge"* (Ephesians 3:18-19).

As we look at The Radical Jesus through the eyes of Scripture we should see ourselves in a whole new light. The only way to rightly know ourselves is to know Christ more intimately for it is that knowledge that will bring spiritual transformation. The practical application of the truths taught in this book can change lives and arouse the sleeping giant called the church. When awakened, she will be a force with which to be reckoned. Hell itself always trembles before an awakened church empowered by the Holy Spirit.

I pray for you as Paul did for the Ephesians, *"that the eyes of your heart may be enlightened in order that you may know the hope to which he has called you, the riches of his glorious inheritance in the saints, and his incomparably great power for us who believe"* (Ephesians 1:18-19).

CHAPTER ONE

Radical JESUS

Jesus is absolutely radical! This assertion is true regardless of the fact that our current church culture attempts to communicate the opposite image of Him. Yet in spite of all our opinions, we cannot alter who He is. Jesus remains the unchangeable God who will never submit to the philosophies or conform to the religious opinions of men. If people will honestly open their hearts and minds to the truth about the Christ, they will be forced to conclude that they are in desperate need of a fresh vision of this Radical Jesus. To believe lies, illusions and mere traditions about Him is neither safe nor honest.

Many have tried to recreate Jesus into a god who conforms to their religious, moral and philosophical beliefs. Their version of Jesus could be anything between a tyrannical deity and an insignificant god that is irrelevant to the existence of mankind. Others try to reduce Him to a mere teacher, prophet or angel. To create in our minds a Jesus who is other than who He has revealed Himself to be is both blasphemous and idolatrous. Whether we like it or not, Jesus refuses to cooperate with our efforts to mold Him into a god of our own making; He remains the radical God-man who Scripture clearly reveals.

Everything about Jesus is absolutely radical: who He is, what He did, what He taught, what He is doing and what He will do in the future. There has never been another like Him, never will be, nor could there ever be. He is the infinitely unique Great I Am who created everything out of nothing and by the *"breath of His mouth"* birthed the *"starry host"* (Psalms 33:6). A God like this is not tame, safe, nor manageable! This is the Star Breather who walked this planet in human form.

Christ's work of salvation is radical! The redemption the infinite Jesus purchased for us is more radical than our finite minds can comprehend. Even so, if we have any substantive understanding of His work of salvation we can only stand in awe of its immeasurable wonders. His sacrifice of becoming a man, with the primary purpose of rescuing mankind from their damnable rebellion, is an eternal mystery that will forever amaze the inhabitants of heaven (Ephesians 2:6-7). Only God could conceive and achieve the unfathomable feat of redeeming mankind. The uncontainable God willfully allowed Himself to be contained in a human body so He could be the Lamb of God to take away the sins of the world.

Christ's humility is radical! The Great I Am stooped down in divine condescension to be supernaturally conceived in the womb of a woman and born through natural childbirth. He chose the path of humility by being born in a barn—a home for cows, donkeys and sheep. The first bed the King of kings slept in was a manger—a feeding trough for animals. The very God who forged out of nothing the star-filled galaxies, entered His own creation to live in poverty so He could give spiritually impoverished mankind the inestimable wealth of Himself. There was no greater gift He could have possibly given to His creatures.

Mankind should have adored the infant Savior who slept in that manger; they should have placed Him on the greatest throne this world has ever known. The One who angels adore and before whom archangels prostrate themselves grew up in obscurity. From time's beginning Jesus marshaled the starry hosts and orchestrated their fantastical dance (Isaiah 45:12); yet He remained the meek and lowly Savior throughout His entire life. He who formed the earth with His hands (Psalms 102:25) worked as a carpenter fashioning the wood and stone He created. Jesus is the only man in history who could have justifiably looked down upon depraved humanity and boasted of His uniqueness and wondrous accomplishments. Yet Almighty God came to this rebel planet in lowliness to be the remedy our sin-laden souls so desperately needed.

Christ's surrender is radical! Jesus came into the world to glorify the One who sent Him. He yielded to the Father every carnal desire a human being can have. In fact, every word, deed, thought and ambition flowed out of His loving surrender to the Father. As a young man, Jesus restrained His natural passions so He could minister to sin-plagued mankind suffering under the wages of sin. When His time of public ministry finally arrived, The Radical Jesus was unleashed upon mankind to do them good (Acts 10:38). He had come to *"save his people from their sins"* and would accomplish that great work (Matthew 1:21). It was the Son's joy to surrender to His Father in everything.

Christ's obedience is radical! When the Father spoke, the Son listened and obeyed. Jesus declared, *"For I did not speak of my own accord, but the Father who sent me commanded me what to say and how to say it"* (John 12:49). Not only did the Savior faithfully say what the Father wanted Him to say but also said it exactly as the Father willed. Such utter obedience is incomprehensible to rebels such as us! Jesus did everything the Father told Him to do, and He did it with burning zeal. He did not think a single thought, speak a single word or perform a single miracle out of self-will. His thorough obedience to the Father assured perfect unity within the triune Godhead as He walked this planet in human form. Our finite minds can easily be overwhelmed with such an incredible mystery!

Christ's touch is radical! The hands that touched hurting humanity were the same that *"measured the waters in the hollow of his hand"* and *"with the breadth of his hand marked off the heavens"* (Isaiah 40:12). When those hands touched the deaf, their ears were opened; when they reached out to prostitutes, they were transformed; and when His fingers fell upon lepers, they were thoroughly cleansed. Those hands of inexhaustible power that formed the universe blessed little children with gentle affection. Yet those gentle hands of tenderness can also be instruments of terrifying justice: *"'You have rejected me,' declares the LORD. 'You keep on backsliding. So I will lay hands on you and destroy you; I can no longer show compassion'"* (Jeremiah 15:6). Jesus is not a manageable deity!

Christ's voice is radical! David joyfully declared, *"The voice of the LORD is powerful; the voice of the LORD is majestic"* (Psalm 29:4) and the psalmist sang, *"Nations are in uproar, kingdoms fall; he lifts his voice, the earth melts"* (Psalm 46:6). When the Lord spoke to Elijah, he was never the same. He must have been alarmed when the wind tore the mountain, shaken when the earth quaked, and filled with dread when fire engulfed the land. When the Great I Am whispered to the prophet with a *"still small voice"* he covered his face in overwhelming fear (1 Kings 19:11-13). All this came from the radical voice of Jesus Christ.

When God incarnate spoke, radical things happened. How could it be otherwise? Just a word from His lips caused the blind to see, the lame to walk and the dead to return to life. Demons shuddered and fled the bodies they possessed when Christ's voice pierced their darkness. Repentant sinners were delivered from lifelong enslavement when Jesus declared that they were forgiven. Multitudes were fed and healed at His word. This was not a different voice from the One who spoke light into existence. It has always been the voice of Jesus, the radical Creator-God (John 1:3).

The same all-powerful mouth that birthed the *"starry host"* spoke the Sermon on the Mount. Christ's teachings were radical because they flowed out of the limitless mind that created everything out of nothing. From Christ's spectacular wisdom came His revolutionary teachings on the kingdom of God (Matthew 13); and it was He who revealed to the apostle how repentant rebels *"may have power ... to grasp how wide and long and high and deep is the love of Christ"* (Ephesians 3:18). Jesus spoke words in human language that are the realities of a kingdom not of this world. The truths He declared have the power to transform and empower sinners to live in His heavenly kingdom while still traversing earth.

Since Jesus is radical in everything that He is and does, then it stands to reason that His teachings must be equally radical. In this fallen world, His wisdom is revolutionary. If we do not understand this truth then we degrade His world-shaking, life-changing teachings into nothing more than tame, moral lessons void of supernatural power.

CHRIST'S ATONEMENT IS RADICAL

The conflict that raged within Jesus at the garden of Gethsemane was a struggle only a God-man could endure and overcome. The agony He experienced there was far more intense than any dread He might have felt over the humiliation He would face, the beatings He would endure or the atrocities of crucifixion. He sweat drops of blood over the consequences of taking upon Himself the thoroughly diabolical weight of sin. Jesus knew what He was doing and why He was doing it and made the choice to be the Lamb of God.

The incredible account of Jesus taking upon His sacred shoulders the vast evil that ruined and perverted the entire human race should cause us to gaze in awe at the Christ of the cross. The fact that we are not awestruck over The Radical Jesus and what He accomplished for us at Calvary proves just how spiritually deaf, dumb and blind we are. Everything about the atonement is radical! When we mortals sincerely strive to understand this truth, we will come to adore our Precious Savior with passionate devotion. Words fail to adequately describe what Jesus did on Calvary because our finite minds cannot fathom the immensity of the work. For Jesus to take upon Himself the sins of the world and become the Paschal Lamb is knowledge worth selling everything to obtain.

As the Son hung on that Cross, He took upon Himself the entire guilt of mankind's sin. At that moment the Son, who became sin for us, faced the full fury of the Father's just wrath. Only God could withstand the wrath of God. For a short space of time the triune God experienced the incalculable agony of separation within the godhead. We could never comprehend the immeasurable implications and expressions of this divine act of love for mankind. Such wonders are beyond the moral or intellectual capacity of men to comprehend. This is truly radical!

The worst curse of hell is not fire, it is separation from God; yet this is the agony Christ experienced on the cross. By taking our sin upon Himself, Jesus received the judgment we so justly deserved. He suffered hell so that no one who would ever place their faith in Him would have to taste its eternal horrors. Oh, what love divine! That God would pay such a price for wretched souls like us is truly Good News!

All of heaven must have gazed in horror as they watched their God expire upon the cross. When He rose from the grave heaven rang with new songs of exuberant joy! The victorious Christ had conquered sin, death and hell! From that moment, the power of Christ's resurrection was available to transform sin-laden humanity so they could be born again into His radical kingdom and enter into intimate fellowship with an infinitely holy God.

The Star Breather is the Hound of Heaven who has, is, and will pursue each and every human being in ways we cannot trace or figure out. He who knows every star by name thoroughly understands the intricate workings of every human being. The Radical Jesus is laboring with His all-powerful ability to save everyone who will receive His gift of salvation. The Lord's magnanimous heart has made it possible for any child of Belial to be transformed and adopted as sons and daughters of the Living God. His unfailing grace is available to anyone who desires to know the Wonderful Savior and become a finite reflection of His infinite perfections.

Adam was God's expression of what a human being was supposed to be. However, sin perverted and marred humanity. From the moment sin entered the world God's original intent for mankind was horribly altered. Our fallen nature has grossly distorted the Lord's original intent about what it means to be human. When Jesus became man, His life and teaching reestablished God's purposes for mankind by making Himself the definition of what it means to be human. Jesus came into the world to reestablish the very reason-for-being of the human race. He accomplished this through His life, teaching, death and resurrection. In fact, in the final analysis, Jesus was the only normal person this world has ever known. Now, He is the sole standard by which we are to define normalcy. The more we become like The Radical Jesus, the more normal we will become according to God's standard.

QUESTIONS

1. Why are even professing believers so uncomfortable with the fact that Jesus is absolutely radical? Do you find yourself being uncomfortable with The Radical Jesus?

2. Why is Jesus absolutely radical?

3. Why are Christ's teachings revolutionary? How will it affect your life to live your life according to His teachings?

4. Why does Jesus alone have the right to establish for mankind what it means to be normal?

CHAPTER TWO

Radical
PLAN

The Lord has a plan for all of mankind—a radical plan to give us *"hope and a future"* (Jeremiah 29:11). The fulfillment of this conditional plan directly depends on whether or not we seek Him with all of our hearts (Jeremiah 29:13). If we seek Him wholeheartedly, He promised to give us the greatest of all rewards—the gift of Himself. Thus, the Lord declared, *"I will be found by you"* (Jeremiah 29:14) and will be *"thy exceeding great reward"* (Genesis 15:1 KJV).

Since God is infinite, the mysteries that surround Him are immeasurable. One mystery (of many) about God is that, in spite of the fact that He needs nothing outside of Himself, He actually seeks out frail human beings who will worship Him *"in spirit and truth"* (John 4:23). What an astounding thought! He does not need us, but He does want us.

A CHALLENGING THOUGHT

Have you ever thought about what it would have been like to walk with Jesus during His earthly ministry years? Though it would have been incredible, we would have also found it extremely distressing. His words, deeds and character would have proved Him a very disturbing individual indeed. He certainly would not be considered a conventional religious teacher.

Understand though, Jesus had no ambition to be some pop religious superstar as is so often the case today with many of our agenda-filled, claim-to-fame, aspiring preachers. The Savior did not perform miracles for the kind of "shock value" that tends to draw large crowds; nor was He motivated to develop a cutting-edge ministry to wow the people. He never took a survey to learn what the local inhabitants wanted out of their religion so that He might offer them a positive religious experience. The truth is that Jesus would be considered a failure by our modern church growth gurus. No, He could never be accused of tailoring His message to make Himself popular. Let's face it: His life and preaching were so controversial that they killed Him.

Actually, Jesus' lack of conformity to social customs probably caused many people to consider Him as being strange and extreme. The majority of poor and middle class people only accepted Him for what they could get out of Him. In the end, many of them cried, "Crucify Him!"

If the majority of laypeople only wanted to use Him, the religious leaders were downright hostile toward Him. They hated Him for breaking their traditions and for intermingling with the rabble and "rejects" of humanity. The very fact that His closest followers came from the lowest echelons of society was one more example of behavior they considered intolerable. It was inconceivable to the Pharisees and Sadducees that the long-awaited Messiah could behave the way Jesus behaved. Even some of His disciples attempted to get Him to be more diplomatic with the religious leaders (Matthew 15:12), but the Lord would have none of it.

On top of all of this, Jesus offended everyone—friends, foes and potential disciples. Take for example the rich young ruler who wanted to be one of His disciples (Luke 18:18-25). Jesus told him to sell everything he had and give the money to the poor. That potential donor left offended, taking his vast resources with him. Then there was the time Jesus explained to a massive crowd that He was the Bread of Life. By the time He finished preaching that sermon everyone—with the exception of His disciples—forsook Him. They thought He had gone too far, He was just too radical.

Unquestionably, most people were amazed at Jesus. This is understandable. He made the blind see, the lame walk and the deaf hear. But why couldn't He be more reasonable in the way He did it? He angered the religious elders by breaking their traditions when He healed on the Sabbath. Then He did crazy things like the time He made mud out of His saliva and plastered it on the eyes of a blind man (John 9:1-7). Another time *people brought to him a man who was deaf and could hardly talk.* He stuck His fingers in the man's ears and spit on the man's tongue (Mark 7:32-33). Many were disgusted at what they considered His uncouth actions. Yet, to the astonishment of all, the sick were always healed.

Jesus' dealings with demoniacs were also very strange. Many of those who were demon possessed writhed in agony on the ground, foaming at the mouth. Of course, such incidents were uncomfortable for people. Then there was the time that Jesus cast a legion of demons out of a man. The demons subsequently entered a herd of swine, who were driven mad and ran off a cliff. Upon hearing of this, the local people told Him to leave their area. Once again, Jesus showed a lack of concern about "building bridges" with people.

As upsetting as it may be to people, Jesus simply does not conform Himself to humanity's idea of normalcy. He won't "dumb down" His greatness to make people comfortable with Him.

A PARABLE

Jesus clearly loved to teach with parables. He used them to shed light on spiritual truths that may have otherwise been difficult to understand or cumbersome to explain. With that in mind, I would like to present a parable of my own for the purpose of illustrating an important point essential to the rest of this book.

Nestled within a lush, secluded valley lived an ancient, undiscovered people. In the course of time, a young couple living there brought a child into the world. This customarily happy occasion turned into a nightmare for the parents and entire clan because the child was horribly deformed. In spite of the infant's deformities, he survived and grew. It was clear to the Village People that he was abnormal. The way he ran, the way he played and the way he worked were all noticeably peculiar. In fact, he even looked different! When the Deformed Child grew to manhood his abnormalities only further served to set him apart from his clan. He was so unlike the rest of the Village People that he just didn't seem to belong to them at all.

When the Deformed Man was a child, the Village People felt pity for him, but when he grew to adolescence, they disliked him. However, by the time he reached manhood, they absolutely hated him. They felt such repulsion toward him that they regretted he was even born.

To understand why the Village People hated the Deformed Man it is important to note that these people were an ancient race of hunchbacks. Not only that, but their arms and legs were twisted and their faces misshapen. Throughout their known history, there had never been one account of a child born without a hunched back and twisted limbs.

The astounding reason the Village People were so horrified by the Deformed Man is that, unbeknownst to them, he was actually born a perfectly formed baby. They simply had no point of reference for such a thing! As the Deformed Child grew into boyhood, his perfections clearly exposed *their* deformities. By the time he reached manhood, it became obvious that *they* were the ones who were deformed. The reality of this caused them an emotional trauma they had never before experienced.

With the coming of that perfect child came the only sure standard of what it means to be normal. The Deformed Man shined a light upon the ugliness of the Village People—the very ugliness they had applauded and reveled in for generations. His existence amongst them awakened their conscience to their own abnormality. His very existence was a relentless, silent reproof of their own ugliness. Rather than acknowledge their condition and seek to learn his more noble ways, they turned their shame into hatred of him.

JESUS-THE PERFECT MAN

I'm sure by now you have discerned the spiritual truth my allegory was meant to convey. The Village People correspond to the human race and the secluded valley, our planet. Their outward deformities symbolize the inward corruption of mankind, which has been exacerbated by the love and practice of sin. Sin, in all of its various forms, literally warps man's spiritual, mental, and emotional being. The Deformed Child represents the perfect Child born of a virgin 2000 years ago. In spite of Christ's perfect life, mankind hated Him so much that they crucified Him.

Everything about Jesus and His faultless life exposes the horrendous evil that dwells within us. We have become so accustomed to our moral and spiritual deformities, that we do not know what it means to be normal. Through our twisted ways of thinking, we actually celebrate our deformities, even to the point of making the most warped people of our culture the stars, politicians and heroes we worship and emulate. Is the church any different from the world? No! We applaud and propagate the perverted dimensions of our fallen nature by exalting some of the most depraved, arrogant, sensual and greedy people to high profile positions.

This twisted thinking has also become entrenched within the church. How often we embrace the world's concept of beauty and are attracted to its deceptive notions of sophistication. How easily we are dazzled by secular society's sensualities. Most Christians are gripped by the mesmerizing hold of the world's entertainment. The media has restructured our morality, redefined the family, reinterpreted the purpose of life and reinvented the church. Yet the more we become like the world the uglier we grow on the inside. This corrupting process only causes us greater pain, alienating us from one another and most tragically, separating us from God.

I did not use the analogy of the Deformed Man to degrade those with handicaps, but to create a visual aide to assist us in seeing spiritual realities to which we are naturally blind. Until we comprehend that our spiritual, emotional and mental deformities are of our own making and the source of our alienation from God, we will never experience authentic spiritual transformation. Just as the Deformed People were helpless to change their outward deformities, so we are helpless to change our inward parts. Apart from God's grace, our rebellion and love of sin will cause us to grow increasingly uglier.

Physical handicaps, as we often call them, do not make a person less of a person. Who and what we are on the inside is what truly defines us. Many people are outwardly beautiful, but inwardly hideous. Though a person may suffer with certain outward deformities, he or she can inwardly radiate a beauty that the majority of outwardly beautiful people will never know.

We will never comprehend what it means to be normal by comparing ourselves one to another. How could we when we're all so corrupted? No wonder Scripture forbids such prideful comparisons (2 Corinthians 10:12). Our hope of change and improvement lies in fixing our eyes upon the only perfect Being that there is, was, or will be. He is the only One who can teach us what it means to be truly normal. The Radical Jesus possesses the sole right to define what is normal for humanity because He is both its Creator and Redeemer. The perfect God-man is our sole point of reference for normalcy.

So how do we rightly define normal? It simply means to be like Jesus. Imitating Him is an integral part of the radical plan God has for us, for without a real resemblance to Him we cannot fellowship with Him or fulfill His perfect will for our lives. We will only grow more like Christ if we seek Him with all our hearts. Just be aware, though, that the closer we resemble Him, the more the world and the lukewarm church will see us as deformed, fanatical and even radical.

QUESTIONS

1. Give reasons why the Village People hated the Deformed Man. Why do people hate Christ today?

2. Why is a Christlike Christian the only kind of true Christian that there is?

3. What does the story of the Deformed Man teach us about our fallen nature? How do you relate to the Village People?

4. Why do we often take some of the most spiritually deformed people and make them the "stars, politicians and heroes we worship and emulate"?

CHAPTER THREE

Radical STANDARD

Through God's self-disclosure we learn who He is, who we are and why humans are estranged from Him. The Word of God is the only faithful and faultless revelation of the one true God and His plan of redemption for sinful mankind. When we understand the crucial significance of the Bible, we will proclaim the Great Reformation battle cry—Sola Scriptura—which means that Scripture alone must define our faith and practice.

At this point, I would like to expound upon three important truths concerning Scripture. First, the Bible cannot save, only Jesus can. Paul clearly taught, *"For there is one God and one mediator between God and men, the man Christ Jesus, who gave himself as a ransom for all men"* (1 Timothy 2:5-6a). The Scriptures lead us to the crucified and resurrected Christ, but they cannot of themselves save us.

Second, the Bible's primary purpose is to reveal God, not man. The Scriptures are a revelation of a holy God breaking into human history. If we corrupt the Word by making it chiefly about man, then we create a humanistic religion that dethrones God and elevates man to the center of creation. Besides, Scripture does not paint mankind in a very pretty light, for we are twisted and depraved.

Finally, the Word purposely presents an unfolding revelation about God, which points to, and culminates in, Jesus. This salvation history begins in Genesis and moves along with fixed intent. Paul wonderfully expresses this idea in the first two verses of the book of Hebrews. *"In the past God spoke to our forefathers through the prophets at many times and in various ways, but in these last days he has spoken to us by his Son."*

God's self-disclosure in the Old Testament traveled along a progressive path of revelation over a long period, through many people and in various ways. However, in these last days the Lord manifested the fullness of His self-disclosure through Jesus Christ. We could think of the Old Testament as an unfolding revelation about God with a prophetic expectation of the Messiah, while the New Testament is the climactic revelation of the Messiah. This means that the primary purpose of the Bible is to reveal Jesus—our God and Savior.

This leads us to two important dimensions that the Word reveals about Christ which are central to a biblical faith. To begin with, the Eternal Son came to seek and to save sinners (Luke 19:10). This is the primary reason for atonement. Next, the very fact that Jesus was *"made like his brothers in every way"* by sharing in our humanity (Hebrews 2:14, 17) reveals that He literally became the standard to define what it means to be human and more specifically, Christian. The Scriptures clearly command believers to live like Jesus. To make anything other than Christ the standard of Christianity is to create a false religion.

The faith that Jesus authored is radical because He is radical. We will not live out this radical faith until we fully believe that Jesus is the only standard for biblical Christianity. Since the inception of Christ's ministry, hell has relentlessly attempted to redefine the Christian faith. As genuine believers, we should never define our faith and practice by man's traditions or pet doctrines. Nor should we allow our faith to be influenced by secular society, as do some of the pop forms of Christianity that abound today. Only the life of Christ, as described in Scripture, is to define the true faith (1 John 2:6; John 13:15; Ephesians 5:1-2).

The majority of professing Christians in western culture are not radical because they have not truly made it their life's ambition to be like Jesus. By forsaking the only sure standard for faith and practice, they are bound to live contrary to Christ and His Word. In doing so, they allow something other than Jesus to define their faith and way of living. However, the more we become like Jesus in thought, word and deed, the more we will turn into true radicals like Him.

It does not take long while walking this faith journey to learn that to live like Jesus is impossible for fallen humanity. Herein lies the miracle of biblical Christianity: to live like Jesus is thoroughly obtainable through Him, but it is through Him alone. It is like walking on water: impossible without the Savior, but completely possible with Him.

A PROBLEM WE FACE

Picture for a moment a man taking a colony of struggling ants out of their harsh environment and putting them into a huge terrarium that is a virtual ant paradise. He supplies them with the finest food and drink ants could desire. He talks to them day and night and endeavors in every way possible to make their lives joyful and fulfilling. Yet when all is said and done, there could never be any viable communication or reciprocal love between the man and his ants. The ants would not know the man exists even though he took constant care of them. They are so dissimilar from one another that they cannot have any meaningful relationship. For there to be any mutual affection between the man and his ants, they must somehow become more like each other.

Likewise, we finite mortals are infinitely dissimilar to the infinite God. He is unique and we are altogether unlike Him. In the beginning, God created mankind in His own image so we could have true fellowship with Him. When sin entered the world the human race mutated into a monstrous deformity, becoming only a vestige of what we once were. Sin had so deformed and twisted us on the inside that we became like the ants, vastly dissimilar to the One who lovingly cares for us. As a result we are unable to have an authentic, reciprocal relationship. It took the timeless work of Calvary to bridge the great gulf between God and man so we could have the meaningful fellowship He originally intended.

Left to ourselves we are hostile to God because our inward deformities make us like brute beasts unable to know Him (Romans 8:7). Salvation is the means by which God "de-uglifies" us through the process of sanctification. As we grow in His likeness, we grow in fellowship with Him. The opposite is equally true: the less we are like Christ the less there will be any real relationship.

HOW TO BE SIMILAR

Salvation is God's gift of grace from beginning to end. How do we become similar enough to Him so we can have authentic fellowship? The Scriptures reveal this comes through self-emptying.* Paul presents this idea in Philippians 2:5-11, which gives us a synopsis on how the eternal Son became a man. Jesus emptied Himself of certain divine attributes so that He could be authentically human while remaining entirely God. Without such divine condescension, there could be no salvation for mankind. Jesus became our atoning sacrifice so we could be reconciled with God through Christ's work on the cross, and thus, have intimate fellowship with Him.

If the self-emptying was only on God's part there still could not be genuine fellowship between God and man because the God-man, Jesus, is infinitely unlike us. While on earth Jesus retained His moral perfections, such as holiness and goodness, which are offensive to our twisted character just as the Deformed Man was offensive to the Village People. Worse yet, our sinful

---

* The doctrine of the self-emptying of Christ and of ourselves has suffered terrible abuse. The abuse ranges from stripping Christ of His divinity to outlandish efforts to mingle Christianity with Buddhism. There has also been an onslaught of erroneous theologies (such as Process Theology) that have further twisted the truths concerning the self-emptying of Christ and the believer. However, errors in theology never nullify the truth.

nature is offensive to God; therefore, man must take his part in a type of self-emptying.

For this very reason, Paul commanded us to have the same mind as Christ (Philippians 2:5). This is radical! Until there is some form of self-emptying on our part, we cannot have intimate fellowship with this holy God. He is working in us to recreate some form of resemblance to Himself so we can have genuine, reciprocal fellowship. This is the process of sanctification. If we want a deeper relationship with our Savior, then we must become more like Him.

To be Christlike we must be empty of self. To be full of self is to be empty of Christ. We are the rebels who cause the hostility between God and ourselves (Ephesians 2:3). Our only hope of enjoying a meaningful relationship to Him is to become more like Him. The importance of this cannot be overstated.

The sanctifying process includes daily dying to our sinful passions and lusts (Matthew 16:24). This is a nonnegotiable condition of discipleship! If we correctly live out the Christian faith, this sanctifying process will continue through our entire sojourn on earth. The more we die to self the more we will resemble Christ, which, as already stated, causes our fellowship with Him to grow. This kind of fellowship is a powerful motivator in our battle with the world, the flesh and the devil.

The shallowness of the present day church is directly tied into the unwillingness of self-professing Christians to faithfully live the teachings of Scripture. By refusing to make Jesus the standard of their life and faith they have rejected His commands to crucify their sinful nature. The love of sin and self has been the eternal downfall of multitudes that will one day be completely separated from Christ's glorious presence. Why do people stubbornly cling to the sins and attitudes that cause them sorrow and ruin?

Here is the importance of holding to the true standard of Biblical faith: since Jesus is the standard of what it means to be human and Christian, and to fellowship with Him we must be like Him, then He must be the consuming object of our lives. Without knowing the written Word we cannot know the Living Word—Jesus. Forsake the written Word, or stray into doctrinal error, and the very person of Christ becomes obscured. How can we be Christlike and not know Christ? Impossible!

QUESTIONS

1. Why is it of such importance that we "proclaim the Great Reformation battle cry—Sola Scriptura"?

2. Why is our relationship with God explicitly tied into our knowledge of His Word? Is it possible to be Christlike without a correct, Biblical knowledge of the Word?

3. What does the self-emptying of Christ mean? What does the self-emptying mean for Christians?

4. What are your thoughts about the analogy of the man and his ants? Why could the man and his ants not have a meaningful, reciprocal relationship? What would it take for them to have one? Now explain why Christlikeness is such an integral a part of having a genuine relationship with Jesus.

CHAPTER FOUR

Radical
TRUTH

Truth will never yield to opinions. It stands defiantly against lies like granite cliffs against a hurricane. Though it is viciously attacked, truth will always emerge as an unconquerable champion; all falsehoods will fall as helpless enemies slain at its feet. You can examine truth, scrutinize it, dissect it, but you cannot change it, for it remains steadfast and unmovable. Truth is fearless, for nothing can topple its throne—as an impregnable fortress, it has withstood the most vehement assaults. Time and again, the self-proclaimed wise have thought they proved truth wrong; in the end, they only proved themselves to be fools. Though you doubt the truth, it remains unchangeable, for it cannot deny itself.

One day Truth had a face and was called by a name.

TRUTH IN HUMAN FLESH

When The Radical Jesus spoke, eternal truths came bursting into a world hiding behind lies and illusions. Jesus boldly declared, *"I am the way and the truth and the life. No one comes to the Father except through me"* (John 14:6). Through this revolutionary statement, Jesus announced to the world His divinity and that He is the only way of salvation. He also established the fact that He literally was the Truth.

None of Christ's enemies could bring a single, legitimate accusation against Him or His teaching. They did their utmost to malign His character and discredit His claims of divinity. But in spite of all their efforts, Christianity flourished. They hated Him for who He was and for what He taught. Everything about Christ exposed the pride and rebellion that formed the foundation of their religion. Jesus was Truth incarnate; His very life offended these purveyors of falsehood.

Almost 80 times in the four Gospels Jesus declared, *"I tell you the truth."* The fact of the matter is that He was a great lover of truth. Jesus never promoted any form of moral or spiritual relativism. His teachings clearly show that there is truth and there is error! Compromise between the two is impossible for they are at war with each other. To hold to the one we must reject the other (James 4:4). Either we wholeheartedly strive to follow the Truth or we will embrace lies. Think of how ridiculous it would be if some people boasted that they based their faith upon 80 percent truth and only 20 percent lies. Yet, such a ludicrous concept of faith has taken hold of a large portion of the professing church.

For people who do not love the truth (2 Thessalonians 2:12) to claim to love Jesus is thoroughly illogical and incompatible with Scripture. Nevertheless, many in the church possess the same attitude Pilate had when he arrogantly asked Jesus, *"What is truth?"* (John 18:38). Jesus didn't throw His pearls before this Roman tyrant, but earlier He made a profound statement that remains true today: *"Everyone on the side of truth listens to me."* (John 18:37)

Genuine disciples will always be lovers of truth—even when it is inconvenient or difficult to live. Such people want truth to permeate their lives at every level—home, work, school, community and church. Above all, they desire it to wholly define their faith. Their willingness to refute the false notions they have entertained in the past has led them into genuine, saving faith. It is this kind of victorious life that allows a believer to boldly proclaim the truth to a world that is naturally antagonistic to God.

TRUTH UNDER ATTACK

Satan's first assault on truth occurred in the Garden and will continue until the end of the age. Some of his deadliest attacks have come through lukewarm and apostate Christians. Such people pervert the Word of God in a vain attempt at justifying their sinful practices.

Jesus, Paul, Peter and Jude ardently warned that in the last days there would be false prophets and teachers that would deceive many. How could this happen? Because much of the church would cease loving truth. Take for example the preachers who get rich off the ignorant and gullible. If the church really loved the truth, these greedy charlatans would not be prospering. Furthermore, there are the popular false prophets who proclaim "*Peace, peace*" (Jeremiah 6:14; 8:11) when God is urgently calling for repentance. These motivational speakers have rejected the preaching of the cross that brings people into saving grace.

Their claim that a person only needs to "accept Jesus" and he will be guaranteed a place in heaven is one of the most deceptive heresies of our time. Such perversion of biblical standards has permeated the vast spectrum of churches, even influencing those who claim to believe in the inerrancy of Scripture. This deception is tantamount to someone believing they can eat rat poison pellets because they only contain a minute (.3%) amount of actual poison.

An example of this attitude can be seen in an experience I had while preaching in a New England church. A deacon handed me a note after a Sunday morning sermon I had just preached. It was written by a young woman who was angry over my message because I had confronted the horrendous evil of fornication that is engulfing the American church. She attempted to justify her own promiscuity by using arguments based upon moral relativism and grossly distorted ideas of grace. Even more tragic was the fact that this woman was training to be a youth pastor in a well-known, two-year discipleship program. Scriptures such as

1 John 3:6 and 1 Corinthians 6:9-10 make it clear that her soul is in danger of hellfire. Moreover, the wickedness she practices will be passed on to the youth she teaches.

Almost three millennia ago, the Lord spoke to Israel a message that the present-day church desperately needs to hear, *"Justice is turned back, And righteousness stands afar off; For truth is fallen in the street, And equity cannot enter. So truth fails, And he who departs from evil makes himself a prey"* (Isaiah 59:14-15; NKJV). The reason the people forsook the truth is because they had forsaken God. *"For our offenses are many in your sight, and our sins testify against us. Our offenses are . . . rebellion and treachery against the LORD, turning our backs on our God, fomenting oppression and revolt, uttering lies our hearts have conceived"* (Isaiah 59:12-13). Israel's abandonment of God brought upon them the worst of all judgments, *"your iniquities have separated you from your God; your sins have hidden his face from you"* (Isaiah 59:2). The modern church does not understand that we are presently suffering under this identical judgment for the same crimes.

Truth has not only fallen in the streets of our nation, it has fallen in the aisles of our churches and on the floors of our homes. How will we ever be imitators of The Radical Jesus if we will not embrace all the truths of Scripture? To pick and choose which truths we want to accept is comparable to telling Jesus that we only like the attributes of Him that make us happy. That is not Christianity, but idolatry; it is creating a false god in one's own image!

In the story of the Deformed Man, the Village People did not have a clear point of reference of what constituted normal until he was born. Since their understanding of what it meant to be normal was so perverted, they could not recognize that the Deformed Man was normal and that they were actually the deformed ones. When the truth of who they were broke into their lives, they rejected the truth because it caused them spiritual, emotional and intellectual trauma. This compelled them to cling to the lies, traditions and superstitions that characterized their community for generations. For all practical purposes, we are no different from the Village People.

We face the same issues in our own lives. The question we must ask ourselves is whether or not we will conform ourselves to the truth as it is presented in Scripture. Truth always forces a decision: either obey or rebel. People can foolishly think that since they embrace those portions of the truth that make them happy, they must be right with God. What will they do, though, when the truth confronts the sin and compromise of their lives? At that moment, they are obligated to repent and change their ways. And therein lies the reason rebellious people hate the truth.

There was a time when Christians knew that sin was wicked; now it is called freedom. We once understood that sin produces sorrow and shame; now it is called enlightenment. We even believed that sin was the path to hell; now it is called the road to personal fulfillment. Our culture is one that values tolerance above truth. No wonder we have become a people that freely embraces lies. Regardless of people's opinions on the matter, sin will always be considered evil by the Lord. Truth is the master that commands us, not a slave subject to opinions or social engineering. The truth is not our property; it belongs to Another. It has been entrusted to us and we must give an account to Him who owns it. For this reason, we must be careful not to diminish or alter it. At the end of the day, everything hinges on whether or not we will obey the truth.

REVOLUTIONARY NATURE OF TRUTH

Paul referred to the Word of God as a sharp, double-edged sword that lays open the whole man (Hebrews 4:12). Every word Jesus has ever spoken is absolute truth. There can be no escaping the penetrating power of God's truth. No matter how the Word of God comes to us—whether preached, spoken or read—the Holy Spirit uses it to show us exactly what we are and what we need.

Since Jesus is the God of Truth, everything He taught attacks and conquers the lies of the enemy. His truth is not some passive, pop teaching that is subject to the whims of men, but an aggressive reality that neither men nor demons can stand against. Jesus never cowered before lies and evil; they cowered before Him. And so it should be with the church. True believers should never hide in their churches. Our Commander and Chief ordered us to advance the truth of His kingdom in the hostile territory of this fallen world.

Jesus desires to infuse His radical truth into the lives of His followers so it is pulsating in and through their entire being. The truth, working through the power of the Holy Spirit, is living, active, powerful, victorious and confrontational. When the Word and Spirit are operating together, they will inflame and empower surrendered vessels to turn this world upside down. Fallen mankind is in desperate need of men and women like Paul (Acts 17:6) who will fearlessly live and proclaim the truth—or die trying!

What would happen if the Christian community really believed, loved and lived the truth? We would see saints living holy lives. We would see a church ablaze with love for Christ and others. We would see authentic revival transform our nation. Christians would become spiritual revolutionaries whom hell would hate and heaven would praise declaring that *"the world was not worthy of them"* (Hebrews 11:38). A study of the book of Acts portrays exactly what this would look like.

God's truth is not radical in heaven; it is simply an uncontested reality. It is only radical on earth because mankind is in a state of rebellion. Believers must align themselves with God's truth; the only other option is to go along with Satan's insurrection. We cannot live in both camps. If we wish to be part of God's kingdom, then we must become conformed to His truth. Then, we too will live radical lives.

QUESTIONS

1. What keeps people from being lovers of truth? What about you?

2. How will loving the truth affect your relationship with Jesus? How will loving the truth affect your relationship with family, work, school and church?

3. How you do normally react when the truth confronts you about sin or wrong ways of thinking? Do you want the truth to confront you or would you rather not have to deal with the feelings of guilt or failure? Why?

4. Answer the question, "What would happen if we really believed the truth and lived it?"

CHAPTER FIVE

Radical
HUMILITY

P ride was the creation of angels. Nothing so malevolently destructive could have been created by mere mortals. Lucifer the archangel mutated into Satan when he yielded to pride and angels turned into demons. After the Lord created Adam and Eve in His own image, the devil labored to fill them with pride, to pervert them into his image instead of God's. Satan knew that the pride which ruined him would ruin them. The result of Adam's fall was that mankind became, in essence, a mass of little pride-filled devils.

One thing that makes Jesus so infinitely unique is His humility. He was not branded with the hellish mark of pride that defines Satan, demons and depraved mankind. Yet if someone ever had the right to be proud, it was Jesus. He was the only God-man who ever existed. Who else but Jesus would have been able to state truthfully that He breathed stars into existence? Nobody but the Savior could have justly claimed to possess the wisdom and power necessary to create mankind. Only Jesus had the right to identify Himself as the One who destroyed the earth with a flood and Sodom and Gomorrah with fire and brimstone. Yet He never boasted of these accomplishments because He came as the meek and lowly Savior.

THE GREAT SELF-EMPTYING

There is nothing special about being human. On the other hand, it would certainly be an extremely condescending act for Almighty God to become human. For God to lay aside His dignity and majesty to be clothed in human flesh would be humiliating and demeaning beyond our comprehension. But that is exactly what Jesus did—He *"emptied himself, taking the form of a servant, being born in the likeness of men"* (Philippians 2:7; RSV). It is not just that He emptied Himself of certain divine attributes so He could become fully human; He humbled Himself even further by taking on the role of a bondservant to serve the creatures He created—creatures, I might add, which should have been serving and adoring Him.

Christ's earthly life began with profound humility. He did not instantly appear to the world in adult form or we would have claimed that He was not truly human. Instead, the Lord purposed for the Holy Spirit to put His seed in the womb of a virgin so the Messiah could be both God and man.

When the time for Christ's birth was at hand the Father orchestrated the events that caused His Son to be born in Bethlehem, the ancestral village of David. It was not into a palace that the Almighty was born, but into the stable of a peasant's home. His first crib was a manger designed to hold animal fodder. There He was laid to sleep among cows, sheep and chickens. The Savior did not awaken into a world filled with the sweet aroma of incense, but with the pungent odor of manure and smelly animals. Could there be a more self-effacing way for the King of Kings to be born?

The Great I Am in flesh and blood grew up in obscurity, learning the trade of a common laborer. He who created wood and stone out of His infinite imagination and power became a carpenter fashioning them with human hands and crude tools. To create the mysteries of the universe Jesus had only to speak and they came into existence, but through the toil and sweat of manual labor He built primitive buildings, furniture and tools.

Angels and seraphim looked upon this God-man, awed by each act and word He spoke. They worshipped Him because of who He was and adored Him for His wondrous deeds. They longed to understand the mystery of mankind's salvation that was unfolding before their eyes (1 Peter 1:12). Yet day-by-day people walked past their Savior-God never knowing who He was nor giving Him the homage He rightly deserved. He lived in obscurity until the day of His revealing to Israel.

Christ's ministry years reveal the humble character of a true servant—He gave Himself away to rescue hurting people (Galatians 1:4, 2:20; Ephesians 5:2, 25; 1 Timothy 2:6; Titus 2:14). Personal fulfillment, fame, wealth and position had nothing to do with His life and ministry because Jesus came into the world to serve mankind, not Himself. Everything the Son did was to please the Father and save humanity from their sin. The Gospels do not reveal a single act of selfish ambition, self-will, greed or pride. The divine glory of the meek and lowly Jesus radiates out of the Gospels—the Creator-God coming in humility to redeem proud and rebellious mankind.

The Savior's teachings and miracles made Him the most controversial person in Israel. People either admired or hated Him. The multitudes that followed Christ had no real love for Him; they used Him for what they could get out of Him. Many attended His meetings to see a good show of miracles or get free food. The crowd that tried to make Him king did so out of selfishness. Their desire for freedom from Rome was so great that they were even willing to follow a crazy prophet to get it. In all this, Jesus maintained His humble character and never forsook the reason He came into the world. He remained the meek and lowly Savior to the very end. Even hell itself was powerless to taint Him with its insidious pride.

The betrayals Jesus experienced would be humiliating to any mortal. They began with Judas, an apostle and friend, who betrayed his Master with a kiss. When the soldiers seized Jesus, the remaining apostles forsook Him, fleeing to save their lives. While the temple authorities held the Christ in the courtyard of the high priest, He watched Peter deny Him (Luke 22:60-61). Only

His female followers remained true to Him. After the Sanhedrin Council arrested Jesus, the multitudes turned against Him. Whether it was within the courts of the high priest or before the Roman governor, the people showed their true allegiance to hell by rejecting their Messiah. They even demanded that Pilate crucify the Lord and have an insurrectionist released instead.

Could there be anything meant to be more degrading than the way the Jewish and Roman authorities treated Jesus? They tried Him illegally, mocked Him cruelly, beat Him viciously and killed Him mercilessly. The agony and disgrace of crucifixion was legendary. Before crucifying Jesus, the Roman soldiers stripped Him naked, shamefully exposing Him before men and angels. The glorious God that archangels adore was despoiled in the most reprehensible manner possible. He allowed all this to happen so that He could be the *"Lamb of God, who takes away the sin of the world"* (John. 1:29).

REVOLUTIONARY HUMILITY

Christ's humility makes Him radically different from the entire human race so filled with devil inspired pride. Jesus came to earth to lay a fatal blow to Satan's work of infusing pride and rebellion into mankind. John stated it this way: *"He who does what is sinful is of the devil, because the devil has been sinning from the beginning. The reason the Son of God appeared was to destroy the devil's work"* (1 John. 3:8). Jesus did not appear so He could gently deal with our sin through some version of positive confession. No! He is not trying to wound our pride but kill it. He came to *"destroy the devil's work"* in our lives in all of its various expressions.

If the first sin ever committed was pride, which Satan perpetrated, and Jesus went to Calvary to destroy the *"devil's work,"* then pride must be one of the primary evils God is aiming to destroy in our lives. Christ humbled Himself so that, through His atoning sacrifice, we could die to our pride.

Satan tirelessly labors to keep the flames of pride burning hot in human hearts because he knows that pride keeps people from repentance, surrender and obedience to Christ. Pride is at the heart of our rebellion toward the Sovereign Lord. And pride is the principle sin that holds back the Spirit's revival fire from burning in our hearts and transforming our land (2 Chronicles 7:14).

Until people grasp the reality that pride is deeply entrenched in their hearts, minds and culture, they will not pursue humility and repentance. Even though pride has enslaved and driven mankind with devilish tyranny, people love and celebrate it. Pride is at the root of strife, the breakdown of families and the ruin of nations. It is at the core of every fight, division and contentious outbreak within the church. Evil prospers when pride goes unrestrained. Yet people glamorize it, promote it as a means to be macho, flaunt it as a sexual enhancement and market it as a criterion for success and power. In all this the church is not substantially different from the world.

The hunchbacked Village People, oblivious to their deformity, are a picture of Christians who are unaware of the ugliness of their pride. They simply redefine it as something other than the diabolical thing it actually is—sin. The truth about them is that their pride forms the motivation for their serving and giving. How easy it is to give sacrificially of our time or finances as long as people acknowledge and praise us—like actors who love to perform before adoring audiences. If they could only see their pride through the eyes of God; He hates it! (Proverbs 8:13).

When confronted with the realities of their deformities the Village People became enraged and took their anger out at the source of their disconcerting revelation—the Deformed Man. The perfections of the Deformed Man exposed their ugly imperfections. This is the reality of our human condition. Rather than longing for the change that only Jesus can give, all too often we hide behind the lies and illusions of our own making. At times, we even grow angry with Jesus when He exposes the pride and sin in our hearts.

So how can proud people overcome the very thing that is mutating them into little reflections of Satan? The process of humbling begins by looking at Jesus (Matthew 11:29). He was the only perfectly humble person this world has ever known. Only by studying Christ, can humans know what true humility looks like. Though there are accounts of some wonderful saints that lived more humbly than the average Christian, nobody can take the place of Jesus as our example. Besides, such saints were only finite reflections of the infinitely perfect Lord.

By studying Jesus, we not only learn what true humility looks like, we also come to the disturbing reality of how pride has deeply rooted itself into our very being. Through this combined knowledge, the Savior leads us to Himself, who alone possesses the power to transform our lives. If we are willing and obedient, the Lord will infuse into our beings the essence of humility. This is soon evidenced by the surrender of our life and will to Christ.

The next step in overcoming pride is simply to repent of it. God's gift of repentance inherently contains within it the seed of humility. To repent we must humble ourselves before God and people. As we walk the path of repentance, humility will define us more and more.

Christ's humility is radical because it is contrary to the entire human race. The meek and lowly Jesus takes twisted people and revolutionizes them by infusing into their character His glorious humility. Through this transforming work, we grow into His likeness according to God's original intent for mankind. That is why humility and repentance make us beautiful to the Lord. They are God-given gifts that transform us from being little devils into what we were created to be—conformed to the likeness of Christ (Romans 8:29).

QUESTIONS

1. Why is pride evil and why does God hate it?

2. What is humility and why does God look favorably on the humble?

3. Why is humility radical in this fallen world? Why is it foundational to revival?

4. What are the expressions of pride that you presently recognize in your life?

5. Read Genesis 3 about Adam and Eve's temptation and sin. What are the expressions of pride that the serpent used to beguile Eve? What were the consequences of their sin? What was the greatest judgment they received? Read 1 John 2:13 which sheds more light on the content of Satan's temptation and explain what you find.

CHAPTER SIX

Radical
SURRENDER

S urrendering to God is probably the hardest thing we will ever strive to accomplish. The idea can be so terrifying that everything within us screams against it. We may give away our lives or wealth for a cause, but we are much more careful about our hearts. If we do extend them to another, our gift is typically encumbered with stipulations and exit clauses. How much more reluctant we are about surrendering our wills to another! We simply do not want anyone conquering us and that includes God.

There are many reasons why we persistently fight against fully surrendering to God. One reason lies in the fact that surrender is contrary to our ingrained instinct of self-preservation. Then we have this tenacious problem with pride; we do not want people to think that we are weak and in need of outside help. The fear of pain is another powerful influence that can cause us to retain control of our lives. Feelings of hurt, abuse and rejection compel us to protect ourselves from further pain. But the strongest motivating force for our persistent drive to be our own boss is self-love. It is as if we have bouts with insanity—we want to stay in charge even when we are self-destructing.

OUR EXAMPLE

Christ's surrender to the Father appears radical because it was absolute. Our fallen nature is so contrary to Christ's that we cannot comprehend what absolute surrender looks like, much less fathom how to obtain it. Rebellion defines our character to such an extent that we have come to think of partial surrender as admirable. More times than we care to admit we act like the foolish Village People who thought their deformities were normal.

As Christians, we can easily deceive ourselves into thinking that we have surrendered everything to Christ when in fact we have not. Through our irrational desire to retain control over our lives, we fight against God to preserve our self-rule. We often forget that He created us to live surrendered to Him. We will never know what it truly means to be human until we fulfill His original intent for our lives.

To have an accurate conception of true surrender we must know Christ and emulate His life. One day Jesus declared, *"Though you do not know him, I know him. If I said I did not, I would be a liar like you, but I do know him and keep his word"* (John 8:55). Jesus knew His Father perfectly and found the life of absolute surrender of inestimable joy. His surrender was the only logical response to knowing the Father as He did. Since Jesus truly knew the Father, He understood that the Father's will was infinitely good and perfect.

Jesus' surrender to the Father was absolute because He loved the Father absolutely. The love and unity within the godhead is infinite and did not change because the Son became human. Jesus loved the Father perfectly because He knew the Father perfectly. If we strove to know and love the Savior more, then our surrender to Him would be far deeper.

The Son's loving surrender meant total conformity to the Father's will. Jesus made many radical statements concerning this aspect of surrender; for instance He said, *"I do nothing on my own but speak just what the Father has taught me"* (John 8:28) and *"whatever I say is just what the Father has told me to say"* (John 12:50). Everything Jesus said and did was the result of absolute oneness with the Father. Throughout His entire sojourn on earth, there was not a single act of self-will. Such obedience and conformity to another's will is frightening to mortals.

Because the Son knew and loved the Father perfectly it was His passion to please the Father in everything. *"The one who sent me is with me"* declared Jesus, *"he has not left me alone, for I always do what pleases him"* (John 8:29). Before time began there was perfect harmony between Father, Son and Holy Spirit. When the Eternal Son was clothed in flesh and blood that same unity continued. It was, and still is, the delight of the Son to do the Father's will. Christ's absolute surrender was not contingent upon an easy life or obtaining certain blessings, but upon His all-consuming desire to please the Father He loved. This should be a powerful motivation in our lives as well (2 Corinthians 5:9).

LIKE THE MASTER

Jesus commands us to live in the same type of radical surrender He displayed, and as our Creator and Redeemer, He has every right to! What else could be considered a proper response to His work of redemption? Many have claimed that striving to live a life of absolute surrender to Jesus is fanatical. However, to those who are growing in their love for Jesus, the surrendered life is the path to His beautiful, holy presence.

Preachers will often ask their congregations, "How many of you love Jesus?" Typically, a majority of hands shoot up in positive affirmation. However, I wonder how many are really telling the truth. Do their lives speak of wholehearted devotion to Jesus or scream that they do not really love Him? The more a person loves Jesus the more he or she will live surrendered to Him. One needs only look at the condition of the American church, with all its contention, worldliness and sin, to know that there is a serious lack of true surrender.

The truth is that people surrender their hearts to what captures their hearts. It is the love of self, in all its various forms, that apprehends the hearts of most people. If someone loves money, then he will surrender to the idol of greed. If the adoration of other people is one's predominant concern in life, then he will surrender to the idol of pride. If a person is obsessed with drugs, entertainment or illicit sex, then he will surrender to the idol of hedonism. Jesus made this point in the Sermon on the Mount. After comparing the pursuit of earthly pleasures to those of heaven, He said, *"For where your treasure is, there your heart will be also"* (Matthew 6:21).

Not only do the affections of a person's heart drive the course of his life, but he will also become conformed to the object of that love. Those affections are so powerful that over time they will actually mold the person into the image of the object of his love. The greedy person will eventually become a miser; the person who is into sexual encounters will become a sex addict and so on. It is love that dictates surrender.

These dual concepts of love and surrender must be considered with an honest heart. In other words, love for Christ must be more than mere lip service! If we truly love Him, our lives will be living epistles of our devotion to Him. That love and surrender will hold us strong against whatever temptations the devil and his world system may present to us.

I recently read an account of devotion that greatly challenged me. In 1914, a passenger ship carrying 130 Salvation Army officers sank after colliding with a cargo vessel. The ship, the Empress of Ireland, had over 1,400 passengers, but stocked an insufficient amount of life-preservers. While a few officers were able to stay afloat until help came, 109 of them were drowned. Not one body that was recovered, nor one victim rescued, wore a life jacket. All the Salvation Army officers, upon finding there were not enough life-preservers, took off their own and strapped them upon others. When met with resistance their response was, "we are ready to die and you are not." They had surrendered their lives to Christ and became living epistles of their devotion to Him.

THE RIVER OF GOD

The Lord gave Ezekiel a vision of a river of life flowing from the temple in Jerusalem that reveals an important aspect of surrender that should be considered (Ezekiel 47:1-12). This river actually began as a shallow creek, but as the prophet followed the course of it, he discovered that it grew deeper: at first only up to his ankles, then up to his knees, then up to his waist, then, finally, over his head.

This vision offers many beautiful analogies of the Christian faith, but I want to deal with only one as it relates to surrender. At first the river was only up to the ankles and standing in ankle-deep water does not require much surrender; with each consecutive increase in the depth of the river comes the need for greater surrender to it or resistance against it. As the river grows, there is the progressive losing of control over one's life. When the water is knee-deep the person can feel the force of the river moving him, but he is predominately still in control. By the time the water is waist deep he has to fight to keep control of his life or learn to flow with the river. But if a person is willing to trust God, he can throw himself into the raging river of His presence. This life of deep surrender is very disconcerting because the believer must give up complete control to God. True surrender puts him in the radical waters of the Spirit where He is in control. That control is ultimately proven by a holy life of loving obedience

This level of surrender is scary because it moves us into the realm of the unknown where we are forced to relinquish control to God. Throwing ourselves into Christ means we lose ourselves in Him but it also means we find a God who directs our lives in the overwhelming river of His presence. To lose ourselves in Him does not mean the loss of personhood or personality, only the unraveling of our twisted, sinful nature. It is there, in the deep waters of His presence, that He can most effectively straighten out our warped natures so we can draw closer to Him.

Of course—in this fallen world—nobody is fully surrendered to God. The ultimate goal of absolute surrender is unreachable in our fallen condition. What the Lord is looking for is our willingness to mature in this vital area of the spiritual life. He will faithfully bring us to different circumstances through life that will require a deeper surrender to His will, a deeper trust in His faithfulness. Just as true is the fact that each new level of trust and surrender brings with it a greater degree of joy and fulfillment.

For many professing Christians, surrender is something they did one time many years ago. But such temporary commitments quickly evaporate when trying circumstances and temptations begin to appear. However, the person who sets himself on the path of following this Radical Jesus will soon discover that he will be required to undergo deeper levels of surrender. Is this life of surrender radical? Yes, just like the Savior is radical. Is it worth the cost involved? Yes, it is worth it all!

QUESTIONS

1. Why do we persistently fight against surrendering to God?

2. What must we do to have an accurate conception of true surrender?

3. We surrender to what captures our heart. What people or things are vying for your affections? How do these affect your relationship with Jesus?

4. How does the Lord help us in the surrender process?

CHAPTER SEVEN

Radical
HOLINESS

O ut of all creation, only the human race received the phenomenal privilege of being fashioned in God's own image. This unfathomable honor allows us to share, in a limited way, certain of His divine attributes. By sharing these attributes, we are able to have real union and communion with Him, which is the greatest gift offered to mankind.

The fact that God created us in His image has nothing to do with our physical qualities inasmuch as God is spirit. It speaks of our inward life which the Lord designed to be finite reflections of His infinite Self. He created us in such a way that we share certain of His attributes such as intellect and free will. However, it is as we partake of His moral attributes (love, patience, kindness, etc.) that we are allowed to enter into a genuine relationship with Him.

But the Lord possesses one moral attribute that is absolutely unique to Him: holiness. Neither men nor angels can be holy in and of themselves. *"For you alone are holy"* is the declaration made in song by the saints who will be victorious over the beast (Revelation 15:4). In their glorified state, the redeemed gaze upon the holy face of God they were forbidden to look upon when clothed in earthly flesh (Exodus 33:20).

The fact that God's holiness does not naturally belong to any created being causes humans great difficulty in understanding and defining it. It is like someone striving to describe the color blue to a person born blind. To press the illustration a step further, it is like a man born blind describing the color blue to someone who was also born blind. Without a legitimate point of reference, the color blue is a meaningless concept. In like manner, mortals, who are *"sinful at birth"* (Psalms 51:5), find it very difficult to comprehend divine holiness.

In spite of our utter lack of this divine quality, the Lord has allowed us to gain a limited understanding of three aspects of His holiness. The first is that God's holiness includes the total absence of evil: i.e., the Lord has never had an evil thought or done an evil deed. This issue is easy to state but hard to grasp because we live in a world filled with evil and suffering.

Interwoven with God's total absence of evil is His moral perfection. This second aspect of His holiness means that He is utterly incorruptible. His moral character is the embodiment of perfection; it is who He is. Because He is morally perfect, He is free from any expression of anything corrupt.

This leads us to the third dimension of divine holiness— that God is totally "Other." This means that He is separate and distinct from His creation. In spite of the total otherness of God, man is constantly trying to pull Him down to our low moral level, to make Him just like us. People do this because the fact that He is not like us makes them very uncomfortable.

TORN IN TWO

To encounter God's manifest, holy presence is indescribably glorious yet frightening, beautiful yet disturbing, attractive yet repulsive. A person may begin to grasp it, but lo, as soon as he thinks he understands it, he finds the reality of it to be too incomprehensible! His holiness engulfs him, overwhelms him, enraptures him and terrifies him. Like Isaiah, the person is undone by His holiness and can only cry, *"Woe to me! I am ruined!"* (Isaiah 6:5). In that moment, one sees how thoroughly unholy he is and wants to flee from Him in dread. At the same time, His holiness is wonderfully attractive and enthrallingly captivating. All who get a glimpse of God's holiness want to flee in terror and yet, there is something so wonderful and satisfying about His holiness that the person feels compelled to cling to Him.

One example of this inner conflict is the story found in Luke 5. After a profitless night of fishing, Peter loaned his boat to Jesus so He could use it as a platform to preach to the multitude on shore. When Jesus finished ministering to the people, He told Peter to go back out on the lake and try again to catch some fish. Probably with a reluctant compliance the gruff fisherman set out in his boat once again. When Peter and his fellow laborers let down the nets they caught such a quantity of fish that the nets began to break. More help was needed to save the catch so they *"signaled their partners in the other boat to come and help them, and they came and filled both boats so full that they began to sink."*

Peter and *"his companions were astonished at the catch of fish."* This miracle caused Peter to fall at Jesus' feet saying, *"Depart from me; for I am a sinful man."* Could a boatload of smelly fish convict Peter of sin and compel him to implore Jesus to depart? No! In that moment the veil which hid Christ's glory from man was parted just a sliver and that glory came bursting through piercing Peter's heart. This glimpse of God's holiness was both terrible and beautiful. Peter was torn in two, while pushing Jesus away with his words he clung to the Savior with his heart. In essence he declared, "Depart from me, but don't leave me. Your holiness is wounding me, but never again can I live without it."

A few years ago, I was ministering at a church in the Southwest and in one of my messages confronted those living in fornication. A woman who attended this church was living with her boyfriend and left the church full of anger. The next day she called the pastor to tell him that she was awake all night, torn with feelings of guilt and thoughts of running from God. And yet, at the same time, she found herself yearning for Him more than ever. Fortunately, the ache for Jesus and desire to have a pure heart won out in the end.

This is The Radical Jesus; the holy God whom creation cannot contain. He was totally Other before He walked this planet and totally Other when He did. He has never been, nor ever will be, a manageable deity. He refuses to go along with the attempts of some to fit Him into their own pretentious boxes. He was radically holy before creation began and will be so when it ceases. Holiness defines Him; it is who He is. Although He did not decrease in holiness when He walked this earth, the Father had to encase the Son in human flesh that men might look upon Him without dying.

Jesus is not the safe, manageable God so many small-minded professing believers fashion Him to be with their feeble theology. His holiness is so great He must humble Himself to look upon creation (Psalms 113:6). This is the same Jesus who died upon the cross: infinite holiness becoming sin for us that we might become the righteousness of God through His atoning sacrifice (2 Corinthians 5:21).

Christ's holiness is revolutionary—it will not leave us as we are. It causes us trauma because it upsets our understanding about God and ourselves. His holiness will either induce us to flee from Him as an enemy or draw near to Him in loving surrender. The wonder of His glorious salvation is that He takes repentant people who once lived as avowed enemies and adopts them as sons and daughters.

HOLINESS AND SALVATION

The holy perfections of Christ can be as repulsive to us as the perfections of the Deformed Man were to the Village People. His holiness can produce in us an internal crisis as it exposes our unholiness. We may throw ourselves at His feet in surrender or crucify Him afresh in our hearts. This holy Jesus demands a response, so we must choose sides. We cannot be His friend and enemy at the same time.

The astounding gift of salvation means that this holy God calls unholy rebels into communion with Himself. This is radical because only holy creatures can fellowship with a holy God. Since neither men nor angels can be holy in and of themselves, God must impart His holiness to them. This can only happen when they are in active fellowship with Him. When fellowship with God is broken, the man or angel loses God's holiness. An example of this can be seen in the fall of Lucifer as well as that of the backslider (Isaiah 14:12-15; Ezekiel 3:20; 18:24, 33:12-13, 18; 2 Peter 2:20-22).

When people repent of their sin and enter into genuine fellowship with God, He declares them holy by judicial decree. Then He demands that they pursue a life of practical holiness. The Lord declared *"You are to be holy to me because I, the LORD, am holy, and I have set you apart from the nations to be my own"* (Leviticus 20:26). Over twenty times in Leviticus the Lord commands His people to be holy. Peter reaffirms this truth in the New Testament by quoting Leviticus, *"Be holy, because I am holy"* (1 Peter 1:16). We would do well to remember Paul's admonishment that without holiness no man will see the Lord (Hebrews 12:14). Our eternal fate hangs upon what we do with this truth. The temporal "benefits" of compromise are not worth the possibility of forfeiting one's eternal soul.

Biblical Christianity teaches that the radical nature of God's holiness must define His people (this is a nonnegotiable aspect of salvation). When His holiness becomes ours, then we will begin to be radical like Jesus. True holiness comes from our relationship to God; it is not a legalistic set of do's and don'ts. Everyone who walks in real fellowship with the Savior will find obeying His commands a joy, not a means to salvation.

A legitimate passion for holiness can only come out of a passion for God. These two motivating desires cannot be divorced from each other. When we wholeheartedly love The Radical Jesus, we will look upon Him as an adoring child does his beloved father. Then with longing desire we will strive to be like Him in holiness and life: to think, talk, live, love and sacrifice like Him. We will want every thought, word and deed to be an expression of His holiness. Then there will be no place for compromise with the world or sin in our lives.

PLEASING THE FATHER

Only Jesus has the ability to please the Father! This statement may grate against our humanistic concepts of Christianity where man is the center of creation, but it is true nonetheless. The only way sinful people can please the Father is for them to allow Jesus Christ to live out His life through them. When faced with such a daunting task, we can throw our hands up in hopeless exacerbation or seek a spiritual revolution. However, the Lord has made provision for this impossibility through the dual roles of surrender and sanctification. As we continue to surrender to the lordship of Christ, submitting our lives to Him, He transforms us into His own image (Romans 8:29) and lives out His life through us. This is a process that will continue as long as we remain in this temporal world.

Holiness, as it relates to mankind, implies two things: separation unto God and separation from sin. These are indivisible and simultaneous! When a person is genuinely born again he is separated unto God and begins a life of separation from sin. In other words, when a person is truly Christ's, he will cease the blatant practice of sin. When Jesus is our better love, we will not want anything to separate us from that place of sweet fellowship with Him; we will want to get every form of sin and evil out of our lives no matter the cost.

No one who faithfully loves Jesus will practice sin (1 John 3). That is a biblical fact! Yet when we do stumble into sin there is a remedy—it is the cleansing power of Jesus' blood which is freely given to anyone who repents. God freely forgives the sins and transforms the character of anyone who will live a life of repentance. How unfortunate it is that people often think of repentance as a negative thing rather than the positive blessing

God designed it to be. It is repentance that allows sinful humans to be partakers of Christ's holy nature.

The man who wants to be holy will live a holy life and no devil, person or temptation will stop him. His love for God will compel him to crucify everything that breaks God's heart and is contrary to His will. On the flip side are lukewarm "Christians" who do not really want to walk with God. They will contrive all kinds of excuses for their compromise and lack of submission to God.

Christ's holiness will forever be radical since it is both foreign to us and infinitely beyond our comprehension. The miracle of salvation is that a holy God can take unholy people and make them holy so they can live in unbroken fellowship with Him. Our God is radical!

QUESTIONS

1. Define God's holiness. Now define what holiness means for true believers. How can sinful people become holy?

2. Why is holiness so necessary to having fellowship with God?

3. Why are we so prone to think negatively of God's gift of repentance?

4. Why do we have to be like Jesus to please the Father? What does it mean if we do not please the Lord? Can a person go to heaven who does not please God?

CHAPTER EIGHT

Radical COMPASSION

W ho are we that God would sacrifice Himself for us? What do we have to offer the infinite Creator that He would pay such an extraordinary price for our salvation? He does not need our wealth or possessions; He is not advantaged by our praise or benefited by our love. There is nothing the Lord needs outside of Himself to exist, for He alone is absolutely self-sufficient. Nor does the Great I Am need anything outside of Himself to be who He is, for He was holy, wise, just, loving, kind and almighty before creation began. All this reveals the unsettling truth that the Lord does not need us. The joyful truth is that He desires us.

Elihu, the young friend of the patriarch Job rightly declared, *"How great is God—beyond our understanding!"* (Job 36:26). Here is a reality from which we cannot escape. Whether we like it or not, God is beyond our understanding in every dimension of His being. Not the least of His unfathomable attributes are His love and compassion. Since His compassion is as infinite as He is, we are helpless to comprehend the depths and heights of this divine love that *"surpasses knowledge"* (Philippians 3:19). Yet all too often people accuse God of injustice because they do not understand how He operates in this world filled with evil, pain and suffering. Humans are virtually blind to the measureless extent of His compassionate activity on our behalf.

We think ourselves knowledgeable about the subject of compassion because we love our family or feel a twinge of pity over the suffering and lost condition of other people. Yet in the end, we have little resolve to do anything of substance to relieve the misery of suffering humanity or rescue their souls. Divine compassion causes the Lord to grieve over our sin, suffering and misfortune, which compels Him to intervene into people's lives for their temporal and eternal good. The cross reveals that Christ's attribute of compassion is a radical expression of His infinite love where He literally becomes the remedy to our lives.

The radical nature of Christ's compassion can clearly be seen in how He went to such unfathomable lengths to rescue a world hell-bent on hating Him. Take for example the first thing Jesus said from the cross, *"Father, forgive them, for they do not know what they are doing"* (Luke 23:34). The Roman soldiers had just brutally beaten and flogged Him. Then they placed a crown of thorns on His head in mocking contempt. They stripped Jesus naked at Golgotha and drove nails into His hands and feet. The whole time Jesus must have looked into their faces as they performed their reprehensible work. Think of those holy eyes. How many sets of hate filled eyes had those same soldiers looked into each time they performed their bloody work? But Christ's eyes were different. They were filled with incalculable love and compassion. I don't know that those men ever forgot those eyes.

"Forgive them" was Christ's compassionate intercession to hold back the Father's just wrath. The soldiers and onlookers all heard those words. What incredible words! And the Savior uttered them in the face of brazen hostility. What the soldiers and bystanders failed to understand was that they deserved divine wrath for their part in this, the most heinous crime ever committed. But we deserve this wrath as well, don't we?

Christ's compassion is not a mere sentimental response to our suffering. Genuine compassion produces action, and the Lord is relentlessly active in seeking to save the lost. He knows His business and does it with exquisite precision.

The Savior's infinite compassion works in cooperation with His omniscience. He literally knows everything about everyone throughout time and eternity. We cannot escape His searching eyes that see all, nor His probing mind that knows all. Divine compassion is thoroughly interwoven with His limitless knowledge of mankind's tremendous need. He knows the real moral, spiritual, mental and physical condition of every person who has ever lived.

The fact that God is omniscient means that it is impossible for there to be any division within Himself. His infinite knowledge of every person indicates that He knows what is true and right in every situation. As a result, the Lord's compassion will never be at odds with His wrath. We suffer such internal conflicts because our knowledge is lacking. That is not the case with God. In addition, since the Lord is righteous and good, He can only do what is right. This is true whether He damns a soul to hell, pardons a repentant sinner, bestows compassion on undeserving people or unleashes His wrath upon a nation.

Here is one area where false teachers grievously err in their pop teaching on God's love. By divorcing divine love from omniscience, they have created an ignorant god that is at war within Himself. Their rendition of His love is nothing but spineless sentimental notions. With one fell swoop they have severed His head of justice from His heart of love and turned His compassion into a gross perversion that winks at sin. They have created a god without moral strength who has goodness without justice, truth that is subjective and love that lacks authentic compassion.

THE COMPASSIONATE CHRIST

One reason Jesus told the parable of the Prodigal Son was to illustrate His compassion (Luke 15:11-32). He portrayed Himself as a father longing for a wayward son's return. When the prodigal finally returned home from his long journey the father ran out to meet him. It is well known by scholars that in ancient Middle Eastern culture it was considered undignified for a man to run. The very idea that this affluent man would toss aside customary decorum to run in such a way speaks of the deep emotion he was experiencing at the moment. He was so taken up with compassion for his repentant son that he embraced and kissed him. He instantly forgave his son's rebellion and threw a celebration for him.

This parable was beautifully depicted in Jesus when, "*filled with compassion,*" He so often touched the prodigals and untouchables of His day. The Savior saw the crowds and, "*had compassion on them, because they were harassed and helpless, like sheep without a shepherd*" (Matthew 9:36). So He taught them how to enter the Kingdom of God, heal the sick, cast out devils and raise the dead. To prostitutes and tax collectors His compassion poured forth in tenderness to rescue them from their slavery to sin. To the self-righteous, He expressed compassion through strong rebukes and warnings in the hope that they might choose to escape the condemnation of hell.

Immediately after rebuking the Pharisees on one such occasion, Jesus agonized over the plight of the people, "*O Jerusalem, Jerusalem, you who kill the prophets and stone those sent to you, how often I have longed to gather your children together, as a hen gathers her chicks under her wings, but you were not willing. Look, your house is left to you desolate*" (Matthew 23:37-38). When He wept over Jerusalem He declared, "*If you, even you, had only known on this day what would bring you peace.*" Then He prophesied the coming destruction of the city and nation by the Romans, "*They will not leave one stone on another, because you did not recognize the time of God's coming to you*" (Luke 19:41-44). Since the people rejected the offer of His love, the Lord would later attempt to reach them through the devastation of their country by the Romans in 70 A.D. Yet, as severe as this was, it was one more expression of His compassion over their lost condition.

The ultimate manifestation of Christ's radical compassion can be seen in the events associated with the crucifixion. One can hear it in the Savior's intercessory plea, *"Father, forgive them"* and be moved by His agonizing cry of rejection, *"My God, my God, why have you forsaken me?"* (Matthew 27:46). Jesus fulfilled His teaching, *"Greater love has no one than this, that he lay down his life for his friends"* (John 15:13). Love and compassion were timelessly wedded in Christ with sublime beauty and perfection.

AMBASSADORS

Since the *"Son of Man came to seek and to save what was lost"* (Luke 19:10), it is the responsibility of every disciple to carry out that same purpose. When we, as Christians, selfishly refuse to reveal His heart to a dying world, He rebukes us declaring, *"Woe to you who are complacent in Zion … you do not grieve over the ruin of Joseph"* (Amos 6:1, 6). By divorcing compassion from love many of us have convinced ourselves that we can love God without extending God's love to others. However, this is breaking Christ's commands to love God supremely and love others as ourselves (Matthew 22:35-40). John, the "apostle of love," would later reiterate this truth in the strong exhortation about love that he gave in chapters three and four of his first epistle (1 John 3:10, 15-18; 4:8-12, 20-21).

Paul also spoke about the believer's obligation to show compassion when he wrote, *"we are ambassadors for Christ, as though God were pleading through us"* (2 Corinthians 5:20; NKJV). Not only is it an obligation to be an ambassador for the King of Kings but an awesome privilege as well. Accompanied with the phenomenal calling to be Christ's ambassador is the tremendous responsibility to communicate His perfect love and pleading heart to mankind. If we are not faithful ambassadors to family, friends and secular society at large, then we send them the false message that Jesus does not care about their sin and suffering. Christ is then disgraced before the world and made to look like an uncaring deity.

Peter taught that the Lord has given us everything necessary so we may *"participate in the divine nature"* (2 Peter 1:4). This promise reveals what we can be in Christ—that His holy nature can deeply permeate our lives, transforming us from self-absorbed individuals into compassionate and loving saints. Professing Christians who don't personify Christ's character are either not authentic Christians or they are simply unconquered. Only when His character defines us, can His Spirit radiate through us to accomplish *"His good, pleasing and perfect will"* (Romans 12:2b).

A Biblical faith will always promote a Christlike character that manifests compassion to others in our daily lives. It is first expressed to our spouse and children and then to our friends and church family. Through God's grace we are empowered to show compassion to our enemies and do good to those who mistreat us. And through compassion we take the Good News to the streets of our cities and villages, to the business world and marketplace. If we are truly Spirit filled Christians, then we will become compassionate messengers of the Holy Spirit for the transformation of this sin-crazed world. We cannot keep silent when Christ's compassion is working through us.

Victory Outreach is a denomination which is defined by compassion for the lost. I know firsthand from ministering at these churches the price many Victory Outreach pastors pay. When one of these inner-city churches is started, a pastor is sent into the streets to win souls one at a time. He goes after the "worst of the worst," sometimes even moving new converts into his home. He does this in order to help free them from addictions and disciple them into the truth. I have known pastors who lived in one room with their wives and children because all the other bedrooms in their homes were filled with former addicts and gang members. With such an example set before them, the new converts come to see that radical compassion is normal Christianity.

As we turn again to the story of the deformed Village People, we see in them the selfish type of love expressed in our modern culture. There were limits to their love, just as there is to ours. Many of us love so long as it is convenient, safe or advances our selfish ambition. Yet, such self-interest does the opposite it is intended to do. Rather than producing the happiness we yearn for, our selfishness inflicts despair and alienation upon ourselves and others.

Compassion can only be expressed through self-emptying, the giving away of ourselves for the well-being of others. Jesus modeled this perfectly and made Himself the standard of what it means for us to be Christian. His compassion is radical and to this we are called.

QUESTIONS

1. When you think of all the compassionate works of Jesus, which one affects you most? Why?

2. Tell or write down a time you showed compassion to another person. What did it make you feel like?

3. Tell or write down a time you received compassion from another. What did that make you feel like?

4. What are practical ways that you can show compassion more effectively?

CHAPTER NINE

Radical
SACRIFICE

Somewhere before time began the triune God chose to redeem mankind from their *"empty way of life"* through the *"precious blood of Christ"* (1 Peter 1:18-19). Long before Jesus was crucified, even before creation itself, the great sacrifice began (1 Peter 1:20). Christ's redemptive work, which divine intellect conceived, will forever be a mystery to men and angels. His sacrifice was so radical we cannot wrap our minds around it. When we look at God's immensity, then gaze upon the Babe in the manger and the Savior on the cross, we get a brief glimpse of the enormity of His sacrifice.

Allow me to illustrate what the Lord faced with the following scenario. Imagine that a young man was allowed to travel 25 years into the future and could see what would become of his future wife and children. Researching into the history of his future family, he uncovers the horrifying truth that his son, who has not yet been born, would brutally murder him. Further investigation into the crime uncovers the fact that his death would be slow and torturous. How would this young man handle this information once he returned to his own time? Would he still choose to bring into the world the son who would eventually cause his agonizing death? Or, would such knowledge cause him to remain childless?

Before creation burst into existence through the divine will, the Lord knew that the only way He would be able to redeem the yet-to-be created human race would be for Him to be viciously crucified as the Lamb of God. It was there, in the limitless mind of God, when the designs of creation were envisioned, that the sacrifice began. The Lord willingly created the very people He knew would brutally crucify Him. For the *"joy set before him"* He *"endured the cross, scorning its shame"* (Hebrews 12:2). What was the joy set before Him? Every true believer! Jesus thought that the cost was worth the prize. This is radical sacrifice!

THE POWER OF SACRIFICE

The power of Christ's sacrifice is as infinite as Himself. It super-abounds with power so that *"through the blood of the eternal covenant"* Jesus was *"brought back from the dead"* (Hebrews 13:20). Since Christ is the God of infinite value and power His blood must possess the same quality. In fact, His blood had more than enough power to atone for the sins of mankind. Since it was an infinite God who made this sacrifice, how could anyone consider such an atonement to be limited? His sacrificial death super-abounds with all the power necessary to save anyone who will fall at His feet in heartfelt repentance.

John the Baptist foretold the power of Messiah's sacrifice *"to take away the sin of the world"* (John 1:29). The Lamb of God would take the responsibility and the penalty for all sins committed throughout time by bearing them Himself. What must be the magnitude of power contained in this blood which could cleanse, not just the sin of one, but of all humanity? After bearing this tremendous amount of sin, it is important to note that when Jesus rose from the dead, he was free from all guilt and condemnation inherit in sin. Through His own blood, sin lost its power to condemn the Savior as our substitute. The same blood that freed Christ from our sin will surely conquer sin's condemning power in all who cry out to Him for mercy.

THE SACRIFICE OF HIS SERVANTS

The disinterested love Christ exhibited through the cross sets the standard for all Christian behavior in this fallen world.

He sacrificed all for mankind and He expects His followers to live the same way. Everything we do as believers—worship, pray, study the Bible, evangelize, do merciful deeds, etc.—should all be done with the same sacrificial mindset that constrained Christ. One Muslim convert to Christianity clearly characterized what it means to be a disciple of Jesus, "Duty before self-preservation—that is a very important principle in Scripture."

Wasn't this the point Paul was making when he wrote, *"Therefore, I urge you, brothers, in view of God's mercy, to offer your bodies as living sacrifices, holy and pleasing to God—this is your spiritual act of worship"* (Romans 12:1). To be a living sacrifice we must surrender all personal claims and prerogatives; we must allow Christ to use us as He pleases. Whether through life or death, ease or hardship, we are to relinquish all our rights to the Lord Jesus Christ.

On one occasion the apostles asked Jesus to increase their faith (Luke 17:5). His response was that a mustard seed's worth of faith has the power to cast a tree into the ocean. Then He shared some insights on how faith and sacrifice should operate together in our daily lives: *"Suppose one of you had a servant plowing or looking after the sheep. Would he say to the servant when he comes in from the field, 'Come along now and sit down to eat'? Would he not rather say, 'Prepare my supper, get yourself ready and wait on me while I eat and drink; after that you may eat and drink'?"* (Luke 17:7-8).

Jesus then asked a very important question that we need to ask ourselves, *"Would he thank the servant because he did what he was told to do?"* (Luke 17:9). In our pleasure-driven, self-absorbed culture we would say, *"Yes, he should be thanked and rewarded for his faithful service and receive a hundredfold blessing because he deserves it."* However, Jesus said the exact opposite: *"So you also, when you have done everything you were told to do, should say, 'We are unworthy servants; we have only done our duty'"* (Luke 17:10).

Most Christians cannot comprehend the servant mentality that Jesus lived and advocated. Their attitude is the direct opposite of what Jesus said of Himself that He *"did not come to be served, but to serve, and to give His life a ransom for many"* (Matthew 20:28). They don't think in terms of serving, but in being served. It is far too costly for our American version of Christianity to be a living sacrifice motivated by loving devotion to God. Personal fulfillment has become the driving force of most professing believers. We will sacrifice if it is convenient or personally advantageous; we will pray, serve, or worship if it is expedient and fulfilling. But if we have to work in the fields all day and then serve the Master afterwards, well, that is simply asking too much. Some Christians would even claim it is legalistic (a great term to throw around when wishing to avoid one's obligations to the Lord).

On another occasion Jesus asked His disciples, *"Who do the crowds say I am?"* (Luke 9:18). They responded with some of the popular explanations. Then Jesus confronted them personally by asking, *"But what about you? Who do you say I am?"* (Luke 9:20). Peter quickly answered, *"The Christ of God."* In response to Peter's declaration Jesus told them what He would suffer in Jerusalem. He then declared, *"If anyone would come after me, he must deny himself and take up his cross daily and follow me. For whoever wants to save his life will lose it, but whoever loses his life for me will save it. What good is it for a man to gain the whole world, and yet lose or forfeit his very self?"* (Luke 9:23-25). Jesus was presenting a few of the nonnegotiable terms involved with being His follower.

It is one thing to profess to be a follower of Christ, but it is another matter to actually live one's life as He lived His. Jesus never allowed any room for halfhearted devotion among His followers; such an idea was anathema to Him. Believers must do more than call Him Lord; we must bow in complete obedience to His Lordship or face the possibility of spending an eternity in hell with all the other rebels.

DAILY SERVICE AND GREAT SACRIFICES

Everything a believer does through faithful service is only that which is commanded of him; what is his *"duty to do"* (Luke 17:10). Followers of Jesus are called to live their lives in continual service to God. One non-negotiable term of discipleship is to live a daily life of making sacrifices, albeit most often small and insignificant in nature. Jesus made this a condition for *"anyone who desires to come after* [Him]*"* (Luke 9:23). There are also those moments or seasons of life that necessitate what we might call "great sacrifices," something no man would do who has not first embraced a life of small sacrifices.

Take for example the story of Jim Elliot. He was one of five pioneer missionaries who lost their lives in 1956 attempting to bring the Gospel to a savage people group in Ecuador. His widow, Elizabeth Elliot, once related an incident when she was interviewed by a reporter after her husband's death.

Before asking his first question, the interviewer opened with a statement about Jim Elliot dying in the jungles of Ecuador when Elizabeth interrupted him mid-sentence. "My husband did not die in the jungle," she stated matter-of-factly.

The stunned reporter replied, "Mrs. Elliot, there is proof that your husband died in Ecuador."

"My husband did not die in the jungle," she reaffirmed.

The reporter grew concerned about Mrs. Elliot's state of mind and attempted to gently remind her that the body had been recovered.

Looking directly into the reporter's eyes she stated, "Sir, you don't understand, my husband did not die in the jungle. Jim Elliot died before he ever went to the jungle. He died kneeling at his bedside in college where he offered his life as a daily sacrifice to the God he loved."

This testimony gives understanding to the spirit involved with martyrdom. The Lord would never have allowed Jim Elliot the honor of laying down his physical life as a martyr if he had not daily offered himself as a living sacrifice during the years leading up to his martyrdom. When we daily offer our life as a living sacrifice to Jesus, love must always be the motive, or it will not be pleasing to Him. Whether or not we are permitted the honor of martyrdom, an amazing transformation should eventually take place inside us so that our sacrifices will cease to be considered sacrificial but instead will be thought of as joyful privilege.

Mark records an account of something I consider to be a "great sacrifice." Mary anointed Jesus with oil that was valued at a year's wage for a common laborer. While she was anointing His feet, He surprised everyone present by declaring, *"She has done a beautiful thing to me"* (Mark 14:6). May we desire to do beautiful things like this for Jesus. Just as Christ's sacrifice was the perfect expression of His love to us, so our lives should overflow with sacrificial expressions of love to Him. That would be the kind of radical sacrifice that would be our reasonable service.

QUESTIONS

1. Have you faithfully labored for God throughout the day in all that you do? Explain how.

2. How much time each day do you give to Jesus in prayer, study, worship and service?

3. Are you laboring in Christ's service to win a perishing world and build up His church for His glory? Explain your answer.

4. What do you think are the differences between fulfilling our reasonable service and performing a truly sacrificial act?

CHAPTER TEN

Radical
FAITH

Faith can only be as radical as the God in whom we place it. Those who serve a wimpy, wishy-washy god will hold very anemic convictions. However, those who follow a glorious, almighty God can believe Him for the miraculous. True faith will always be radical because the object of that faith is The Radical Jesus.

While examining The Radical Jesus we have established that He is the standard for what it means to be human, normal and Christian. But how do we make Jesus the perfect example of faith? Can He, as God Incarnate, have faith? The self-proclaimed "Word of Faith" teachers claim that God's faith rests in His word. However, if God places faith in His word, then His word stands outside of Him, something that is impossible since God is absolutely indivisible. A further problem arises if we consider that whatever God puts His faith in would need to be something at least as great as Himself. If that were the case, He would be but a lesser deity.

Though we cannot use the faith of Jesus as an object lesson since He operates through divine fiat (i.e., God's creative command), there is still an important characteristic of faith Jesus wants us to learn—that faith and knowing God are inseparable. The Savior commands us to *"Have faith in God"* (Mark 11:22). This is the duty of creatures to the Creator. Unbelief is the byproduct of not knowing God, or of not knowing Him well enough to truly trust Him. When we look at the heroes of faith extolled in Hebrews 11, we find faith that was contingent upon knowing God enough to trust Him. This is the radical kind of faith that we are commanded to live out.

Probably the best way we can address the issue of faith in relation to The Radical Jesus is to study those He praised. The fact that Jesus commended certain people for their faith should intrigue us since He was very sparing with His compliments. Those who had great faith were at the top of His list.

One example is the disconcerting story of the Canaanite woman found in Matthew 15:22-28. Her daughter was *"suffering terribly from demon-possession."* In desperation, she implored Jesus to heal her daughter. What was Christ's response? He ignored her. When the disciples were worn out with her pleadings, they urged Him to *"send her away."* He finally answered her saying that He was not sent to the pagans but to the *"lost sheep of Israel."*

The Canaanite woman then fell at Jesus' feet begging Him to help her. At this point, He made a very derogatory statement, *"It is not right to take the children's bread and toss it to their dogs."* To call a person a dog in ancient Middle Eastern culture was a serious insult. Not only did she overlook Christ's insult, but she actually agreed with His declaration. Now isn't this an integral part of faith, to know Christ and affirm what He says is true even if it seems offensive, negative or contrary to our understanding?

Undaunted in the face of such seeming rejection, this simple woman refused to be denied. Humbly she replied, *"Yes, Lord, but even the dogs eat the crumbs that fall from their masters' table."* In essence, she declared, "I agree with you. I am no better than a dog. I do not deserve your help. I am not coming to you because I deserve it; I am coming to you for mercy. I know that you are good and kind. So I trust that you will come to my rescue."

In this situation neither the woman, nor even the disciples, understood what Jesus was really striving to accomplish. Before He would heal the woman's daughter, which He longed to do, He wanted to help her faith to mature. So Jesus used these circumstances to move the woman from passive belief to radical, miracle-experiencing faith.

Notice that, unlike the arrogant declarations one hears from "Word of Faith" teachers, her faith was expressed in humble trust in a loving God. The fact stands out that the Canaanite woman knew the Lord better than most Israelites. He granted her request declaring for all to hear, *"Woman, you have great faith!"* Her daughter was *"healed from that very hour."* Radical faith accomplishes that which it seeks because it focuses upon the One who never fails.

Matthew chapter eight provides a similar story of true faith. It is an account of a Roman centurion whose servant was paralyzed and dying. He loved this servant and implored Jesus to heal him. In his case, his faith was demonstrated through an understanding of military authority. Being a soldier, he knew both how to give and follow orders explicitly. What stood out to this military man was that Jesus had authentic authority—that whatever He commanded happened.

It was not that the centurion had faith in faith itself, as if he could make something happen through a positive mental attitude. Nor did he believe there was some magical power in speaking out a positive confession, as if saying the right words would force God to heal his servant. The centurion understood that Jesus had authority and what He spoke by divine fiat would be accomplished. In other words, the efficacy of his faith was not in his words, but in the One who has absolute authority.

As with the Canaanite woman, here again the supplicant came humbly to Jesus *"asking for help."* His acknowledgement of personal helplessness was, at the same time, a declaration of total dependence upon God. A believer cannot exercise faith in God if he is trusting in himself or other people. Self-sufficiency is not only faithless, but it is also rebellious and prideful. It is important to note that faith incorporates a true-life understanding of one's humanity and fallen condition. Only when a person grasps the truth of his neediness will he ever really put trust in Almighty God. It's at this point that the Lord stoops down to help His child.

When the centurion focused on the correct object—Jesus—then the miracle happened. When Jesus heard the centurion's statement of faith, "*He was astonished and said to those following him, 'I tell you the truth, I have not found anyone in Israel with such great faith.'*" Even the apostles did not have "*such great faith.*" In our modern era, Jesus is looking for believers to operate with the centurion's kind of radical faith.

THE NEED OF GREAT FAITH

The very sins that deform our character also corrupt our faith. This is why we are in desperate need of a spiritual revolution. Until we are inwardly transformed, our faith will be a perversion of what God designed it to be. The tragic reality of our day is that what most would consider as "*great faith,*" God would see as merely normal. Authentic faith only appears radical because the majority of what we call "*faith*" is so subnormal that it is not faith at all.

Both the church and the world are in dire need of Christians who will truly believe in this God of miracles. It would be good for all of us to remember that without faith we cannot please God (Hebrews 11:6). This kind of trust in God will often exhibit itself through healing the sick, rescuing the perishing and setting the captives free. Without it, Christians will find themselves to be increasingly irrelevant in a world of great need. Radical faith will live and die trusting Jesus.

Nevertheless, even sincere believers are subject to bouts of doubt and unbelief. Then there is the innate self-love that makes a person so consumed with personal comfort that he is unwilling to extend himself to others. It is impossible to live by faith when one goes through life determined to avoid difficulty and pain. Radical faith contains a daring element; it is willing to step outside of what is comfortable, familiar and safe to trust God.

It is as if the Lord is continually attempting to move us to the edge of a great precipice. When we see that daunting cliff, we struggle frantically to stay as far away from the edge as possible. The drop is enormous, and we are terrified at its sight. Still, He maneuvers us right to the very edge of it. With our toes hanging over the rim we quake in fear and wonder why a good God would lead us to such a dangerous place. Then His voice whispers words that cause us to tremble from head to toe: "Jump off, my child, and I will catch you."

The voice of Self screams out in fear, "He's not trustworthy! Save yourself!" The voices of the world warn us of doom and ruin. Demons add their horrifying forebodings. Our knees go weak and we want to run as far away from that precipice as possible.

Then the sweet voice of Jesus speaks again, "Trust Me child and jump. I have never lost one who trusted Me." With trembling knees, we close our eyes and jump. To our amazement, there is no impact; only the reassuring feeling of God's strong hands as He draws us into His bosom.

Though at times disconcerting, faith remains the safest place to be because it allows us to rest in Christ's tender embrace. Without such precipices in our lives, we will never know how wonderful and mighty our God is, nor will we ever have the joy of seeing His miracles operate for us and through us.

Radical faith is about surrendering to the One who calls us to jump into His arms of unreserved love. It compels us to trust and obey even when it seems contrary to our emotions or reason. This kind of faith is rooted in a firm relational knowledge of who Jesus is and what He promises to do. Wholehearted, persevering faith is the only reasonable response for true believers. Such faith acknowledges God is good and will only do good (Psalm 119:68). This is the total trust in and dependence on God that caused the early church to turn the world upside down even in the face of severe persecution. As Leonard Ravenhill so aptly stated, "Faith links our impotence with His omnipotence."

QUESTIONS

1. How does our view of God affect our faith? Think about both the negative and positive aspects of this.

2. What are your thoughts on the following statement: "Wholehearted, persevering faith is the only reasonable response for true believers who know Christ."

3. Do you have some personal testimonies of your faith producing results? Share them or write them down. What do you need to do to see your faith grow?

4. Do you have great faith like the Canaanite woman and Centurion or the little faith of those first disciples?

CHAPTER ELEVEN

Radical PRAYER

J esus prayed as no mortal has ever prayed. His times of prayer with the disciples bore no resemblance to the dry, boring and lifeless prayer meetings witnessed in many churches today. One can only imagine what the disciples experienced during such times. When the Eternal Son poured out His heart to His Father—the heart of God communing with the heart of God—it must have left them weeping uncontrollably.

They surely must also have witnessed Jesus agonizing in prayer over the stubborn, unrepentant sinners who heard His preaching and saw His miracles. How He longed to be the remedy to their sin-laden lives, to deliver them from the cruel slavery they suffered serving hell's taskmaster. Jesus must have expressed unspeakable joy to His Father every time some lost soul repented or some prodigal came running home.

Then there were the times when Jesus expressed His great love for His Father and reveled in their relationship. Those disciples must have had some phenomenal experiences.

Christ's prayers were always radical. For instance, He never approached God with a selfish agenda. His supplications were driven by disinterested love and divine compassion.

Although we can read and study Christ's prayers recorded in the Gospels, we cannot experience the same Spirit-charged atmosphere that His praying must have produced. His words pulsated with the same power He used to speak the worlds into existence. His were not stoic prayers—they were alive, vibrant, penetrating, soul stirring utterances flowing out of the depths of

His divine being. They were not formal lists or written prayers uttered day-in-and-day-out in worthless repetition. When Jesus spoke, heaven stood at attention. Angels and seraphim waited in excited anticipation for the commands that would come from the Almighty who was clothed in human flesh.

When Jesus prayed the Father also listened. The perfect unity and love within the triune Godhead assured Him free access to the Father. But this was a two-way communication. The Father also spoke to Him. The Father and Son lived in continual unbroken fellowship, yet they also enjoyed daily times alone; the two of them together, with no distractions.

No one has understood prayer like Jesus understood it. Not only did He know how to pray, but, as God, He also understands the type of supplications that will be answered.

MINISTERS AND PRAYER

If there was one thing Jesus understood it was that the effectiveness of prayer is directly tied to a believer's relationship with God.

The history of the church offers many examples of this. Those saints who knew how to move heaven first lived in close proximity to their beloved Lord. They had entered Christ's school of prayer and learned how to draw near to God. They were like Abraham of old who agonized over those who would perish in fire and brimstone. They were like John who leaned his head on the Savior's bosom and heard His heartbeat. They were like Paul whose mighty intercessions opened new regions to the Gospel.

To be a Christian means that a person has entered into relationship with God. It is impossible to have an ongoing relationship with little or no communication. How much more so is the case of those who would represent God to a dying world? Those who are in formal ministry but not in constant communion with the Lord are not men and women of God.

They have no business representing themselves as such. The size of one's church, ministry or income is not a proof of their true relationship with Jesus. Hosting a show on Christian media or pastoring a mega-church does not equate to walking with the Lord. Only a person of prayer can be called a man or woman of God. Period! There are no exceptions! There are no short cuts!

Men and women of God are made on their knees, not in Bible school or seminary. Education may provide a person with helpful knowledge for ministry but it, in itself, does not qualify a person for ministry. The truth of the matter is that those who have failed in the school of prayer have failed in every aspect of ministry and even in the Christian life. To be a man or woman of God one must be like Jesus, which means being much in prayer. When the life of God is pulsating through someone's inner being, then prayer will be a driving force in his life.

CHURCHES AND PRAYER

In the same way, one can gauge the spiritual vitality and strength of a congregation by the amount of time it spends in quality prayer. Churches and denominations rise or fall according to their prayer life. A prayerless congregation is a backslidden congregation—made up of numerous backslidden Christians. The life-signs of a church are not found in the size of its Sunday service but its prayer meeting. Prayerless churches are dead churches, whether the size of the congregation is 10 or 10,000. It is operating in the flesh, not in the Spirit. A prayerless congregation that is running a strong benevolence ministry or various outreaches is only doing social work. In His messages to the seven churches of Revelation 2 and 3, the Lord clearly debunked the notion that He is pleased with a congregation just because it is large and thriving.

Prayerless churches are detrimental to the kingdom of God. Their plans and programs originate in the carnal minds of men and are therefore powerless to help anyone. The churches that please Him are those that are crying out to Him on behalf of those in need. Those are the congregations who change eternity.

In the mid-1990s, I was blessed to experience firsthand a revival that changed eternity. The Holy Spirit was tangibly present so the lost were saved, backsliders repentant and church folk convicted. There were many opinions on why the Lord visited this particular church, but the question was answered for me when I heard a comment made by the pastor. For years in this church, a group of women met weekly and prayed for one thing: revival. These women were summoned home before they saw the results of their intercession, but true prayers do not die with the saints that uttered them. The foundation of prayer was laid and the work would be accomplished. A praying church is the only kind of church that can do God's work.

BELIEVERS AND PRAYER

The Lord expects every believer to have an ongoing, vibrant devotional life. He is not interested in meaningless repetitions, lifeless prayers or dead worship. Dispassionate prayer meetings and apathetic worship services scream that Christ is unworthy of passionate pursuit; they telegraph to the world that the Christian faith is not worth living, much less worth dying over. The low view of God that is currently held in much of the church has produced this apathetic level of devotion. It is an insult to God and a disgrace before a perishing world that professing Christians can scream and shout over ballgames and be bored about the things of God!

Prayerless "Christians" operate in the flesh, love the flesh and promote the works of the flesh. Since they love the world, they think and act like the world. When their marriages break down you will always find prayerlessness at the core of their problems (people who dwell close to Jesus have wonderful marriages). Their prayerlessness and compromise disgraces Christ before their children, family and friends. All these things, and even more, are the result of not being like The Radical Jesus who dwelt in constant communion with His Father.

Prayerless people are independent people—they do not see their desperate need for God. This causes them to live without divine help. As the deformed Village People were outwardly twisted, prayerless people remain inwardly twisted; they refuse to live a life dependent on God as manifested by little or no prayer (Psalms 121:1).

The very idea that people are prayerless proves they do not love God, and therefore, cannot be truly Christian. If they truly loved Jesus they would want to be with Him. They may have sentimental feelings towards God, but not authentic love that is always proved through our actions.

RADICAL ABIDING

The Scriptures clearly teach that Jesus lived His life abiding in the Father (John 14:11). Forty-seven times in the Gospel of John, Jesus stated in one way or another that whatever He said or did was done solely within the parameters of the Father's will. He was utterly dependent upon, and completely submitted to, the Father.

It is difficult for finite minds to grasp the tension between the humanity and divinity within Christ and even more so to comprehend the relationship between the Father and Son. Paul briefly addressed this when he wrote, "Who, *being in very nature God, did not consider equality with God something to be grasped, but made himself nothing, taking the very nature of a servant, being made in human likeness*" (Philippians 2:6-7).

Paul's statement reveals the fact that Jesus was wholly God and wholly man. The difficult phrase *"did not consider equality with God something to be grasped"* teaches us that Jesus, being equal with God the Father, did not insist on retaining His divine right as God. He laid aside His prerogative to use those rights and for a time became wholly dependent upon the Father.

The willingness Jesus showed to live in such dependence and submission is what it means to abide in God. Jesus showed in many different ways that He was unwilling to step outside of God's will in any way. We see this demonstrated in the Savior's prayer life when He went up on the mountain to pray through the night before choosing His disciples (Luke 6:12-13). His prayer life was one aspect of His abiding life.

The believer who lives in true dependence on God has within him a consistent yearning to spend time with the Lord on the mountain. The results of this kind of life will be manifest in the quality and quantity of the believer's prayer life. Such people will pray much because the Lord alone is their *"exceeding great reward"* (Genesis 15:1).

The abiding life is only for those who are weak in themselves and realize that all they need will be found in Christ. Because they are continually aware of their spiritual poverty and desperate neediness, they willingly allow the Lord to do everything in them and through them. Jesus said, *"Abide in me, and I in you. As the branch cannot bear fruit of itself, except it abide in the vine; no more can ye, except ye abide in me"* (John 15:4; KJV). A branch cannot live apart from the vine. Spiritual life only comes through Jesus. When fully attached to Him, the believer receives the life that Jesus alone can give; being cut off from Him can only bring spiritual death.

As branches who are dependent on the vine, it is necessary that we lay aside our rights, desires, ambitions, gifts and talents in the same manner Jesus did. Every form of self-will and self-sufficiency must be prayerfully surrendered. We must even be willing to die to things that Scripture does not consider "sinful"—those things that keep us from abiding in Christ—regardless of their apparently innocent nature. We are called to this level of devotion even if it seems excessively radical. We will never be willing to live this way if we are not people of prayer.

The other image presented in Jesus' illustration is that the purpose of the branch is to produce fruit that displays the glory of the Vine. Everything, including the painful pruning, is meant to accomplish this end. The obvious condition to abiding in the vine is to consider oneself as nothing but a branch which exists only for His glory.

To abide in Christ literally means a person gives up everything for Christ—but it also means that he finds everything in Christ. What can compare to that intimate fellowship with Jesus one is allowed to enjoy as he dwells in Him? Psalm 91 promises that, *"He that dwelleth in the secret place of the most High shall abide under the shadow of the Almighty"* (Psalm 91:1 KJV). The very idea of abiding in Christ denotes nearness to Him. Many Christians live unfulfilled lives, not because Jesus cannot satisfy their dry, weary souls but because they do not dwell with Him in the secret place. They have deemed this kind of life too costly, too extreme.

The One whose eyes burn like *"blazing fire"* (Revelation 1:14) expects His followers to live and pray as He did. His prayer life was led by divine purpose, burned with passion and operated in humble submission to the Father. Oh Lord, teach us to pray!

QUESTIONS

1. Why are prayerless "Christians" not true Christians?

2. How does our view of God affect our prayer and worship? Think about the difference between a low view of God and a high view of Him. (Isaiah 6:1-5)

3. Why are prayerless people and churches detrimental to the kingdom of God? Why are believers that are much in prayer the only ones that can effectively advance the kingdom of God?

4. How do we abide in Christ?

CHAPTER TWELVE

Radical
PURSUIT

The Lord seeks mankind with a tenacious passion. As the Hound of Heaven, He relentlessly pursues people. In fact, the Bible is the unfolding wonder of God's self-disclosure to sinful mankind. The pinnacle of this marvelous story was the Eternal Word becoming human. It was the ultimate expression of divine love to a world bent on practicing evil. What can be seen in the Scriptures, and in a broader sense of all history, is God's persistent pursuit of man.

When humanity's first parents sinned and attempted to hide themselves from God, He called out to them, *"Where are you?"* (Genesis 3:9). The Lord had not lost Adam and Eve; He knew exactly where they were. They had lost themselves in sin and God was pursuing them. Thus began the divine chase of every soul that would come into the world.

The Scriptures are full of accounts of people who the Lord aggressively sought. The results of those divine chases are as diverse as the stories themselves. Some were saved, others were judged, a great number found deliverance, while many suffered bondage. Beginning with Adam and flowing through history to Abraham and then on through Moses and the nation of Israel, the Lord revealed His wonderful, and at times, terrifying love. Whether He used a still small voice to shake a prophet or a pagan army to devastate His rebellious people, it was God pursuing man for their eternal good. He never grows weary, never slumbers or sleeps. This ever-present, all-powerful God is perpetually busy about His work of saving everyone who desires redemption. He knows exactly what is necessary to bring rebels to salvation and will do everything that is in keeping with His character to accomplish the task.

In the 1930s, Joseph Stalin attempted to purge Russia of every Bible and every Christian. This was the case in Stavropol, Russia, in which thousands of Bibles were confiscated, and multitudes of believers were condemned as "enemies of the state" and sent to die in Siberian prison camps.

Years later, when the iron curtain was lifted, a mission organization sent a team to Stavropol. Just when they were confronted with the problem of obtaining Bibles for the people, they learned of the existence of a warehouse outside of town where the confiscated Bibles had been stored since Stalin's time. The team gave themselves to prayer, requested and were granted permission to distribute the Bibles to the people.

The next day they hired some young men to help load the Bibles into a truck. One of the young men was a college student hostile to the gospel who came only for the day's wages. As they were loading Bibles, a team member noticed that the young man was missing. Eventually he was found in a corner of the warehouse, weeping. This young man had taken one of the Bibles, hid in a corner of the warehouse and opened it out of curiosity. In that moment, he caught a glimpse of the God who pursues.

What he found in that Bible shook him to the core. The inside cover had the signature of his own grandmother. It had been her personal Bible—a woman who, throughout much of her life, had been persecuted for her faith. Out of the thousands of Bibles in that warehouse, he stole the very one belonging to his grandmother!

We can only comprehend a small portion of the Savior's radical pursuit of mankind. The infinitesimal ways in which Jesus sacrificed Himself so that He could adopt as sons and daughters those who were once His enemies is thoroughly amazing. The apex of this divine pursuit is unveiled through the gruesome scenes that began in the Garden of Gethsemane, progressed through the scourging He received in the Roman Praetorium and culminated on Mount Calvary where He was murdered. The Lord of Glory openly displayed before the world His aching heart to redeem wayward mankind throughout the events of that fateful day. *"Can a mother forget the baby at her breast and have no compassion on the child she has borne? Though she may forget, I will not forget you! See, I have engraved you on the palms of my hands"* (Isaiah 49:15-16). His nail pierced hands and feet will be eternal emblems of His passionate pursuit of mankind and a perpetual reminder of God's unfailing love.

MAN'S RESPONSE TO GOD'S PURSUIT

Christ's pursuit of mankind is thoroughly radical. Man's pursuit of God should display that same passion. How often, though, is that the case? Most people respond to His loving overtures with indifference. *"I spoke to you again and again, but you did not listen; I called you, but you did not answer"* (Jeremiah 7:13b). In spite of man's willful ignorance of His love and all the ridiculous lies people have hurled at Him, He presses on with deliberate, persistent desire.

Yes, He loves mankind with a radical love beyond comprehension. He pursues people with urgency because He knows our lives on earth are as a vapor, here today and gone tomorrow. He knows we desperately need Him. The Lord is ever laboring to compel people to the foot of the cross. He uses whatever means that are at His disposal in His attempt to win man's devotion: physical suffering, loneliness, depression, as well as the painful consequences of sin.

Oh, how foolish it is when people run away from Him! They fight against the One who can do infinite good to them. They run to the very things that incur ruin and misery. The life of the typical self-proclaimed Christian today is full of worldly distractions they turn to: television, video games, internet, sports, money, sex, drugs, recreation and so on. It all reflects empty lives that have little interest in God. They are too busy for church, too busy to pray, too busy to study God's Word and too busy to evangelize. Much of the church has become a self-absorbed, pleasure-driven, selfish people who claim to love God while actually being in bed with the devil.

How can people say they love Jesus and not respond to His love? Wouldn't their professions of devotion be empty and meaningless? Think of a young man who passionately longs to marry his beloved. She has openly committed herself to this relationship; indeed, she is wearing the engagement ring he purchased for her. How would that young man feel if he found out that his bride-to-be is actually in love with his archenemy? Would this not be an offense of horrendous magnitude? Would this not break his loving heart and justify his righteous anger? But this is exactly what a large portion of professing believers do all the time to Jesus. They claim to love Christ and desire all of the benefits associated with such a relationship. And yet, a look at their daily lives reveals the undeniable fact that they have given their hearts to the very things that make up the kingdom of this world. At best their love for Him is halfhearted; at worst, it is entirely absent.

Jesus did not radically pursue people so that they might become spiritual whores. The Lord's judgment of Jerusalem through Nebuchadnezzar is an example of His reaction to such spiritual adultery. The Lord declared through Isaiah, *"See how the faithful city has become a harlot!"* (Isaiah 1:21). He later made a similar statement through the prophet Hosea: *"Their deeds do not permit them to return to their God. A spirit of prostitution is in their heart; they do not acknowledge the LORD"* (Hosea 5:4). Israel's sin was not just what they did, but what they had fully become, for *"a spirit of prostitution"* had filled their hearts. The lies they believed about the Lord and about the pagan idols they worshipped kept them from returning to the Lord.

Much of the American church is in a similar position with the Lord. They claim to be His people all the while they are prostituting themselves with the world. Their halfhearted devotion keeps them living between two worlds while all the time believing the lie that they are right with God.

Only deep, heartfelt repentance will bring about the transformation of hearts and lives that is needed. Only an aggressive commitment to break off all associations with the enemy will allow people to possess a real life in God. I fear that many professing Christians are quickly heading into eternal judgment.

MAN'S PURSUIT OF GOD

Of course, repentance indicates a change in thinking and a new direction in life. As true believers, we must work to develop the kind of heart that will radically pursue Christ. Once we have recognized the truth of our adulterous hearts, every idol of the heart must be destroyed. To develop a heart that radically pursues Christ we must have a love for God that is greater than our love of the world.

A wonderful expression of the pursuit of God is found in Psalm 73. We find Asaph struggling with the apparent injustices of life. He observed the righteous suffering adversity while the ungodly were enjoying prosperity. However, all that changed when he entered God's sanctuary. Only in the spiritual temple, where His glory dwells, are the things that really matter made clear. The result of this revelation is expressed in verse 25, "*Whom have I in heaven but you? And earth has nothing I desire besides you.*"

Following hard after Jesus forces one to make daily choices to pursue Him rather than the things of earth. I recall reading a statement several years that impacted me regarding this subject. This man of God urged those desiring a life of radical pursuit to "narrow your interests." To narrow or limit our interests forces us to take great pains to keep our lives clear of unnecessary clutter. As the thought, *"Earth has nothing I desire,"* consumes our heart, the clutter demanding our attention is treated as a thief attempting to steal our most valuable treasure.

Jesus must be the prize of our lives, the One we seek above everyone and anything. He must be the destination of our lives and the road by which we arrive there. We must move beyond fanciful ideas and sentimental notions to the place where we will not let suffering nor prosperity, life nor death, angels nor demons, *"separate us from the love of God that is in Christ Jesus our Lord"* (Romans 8:38-39). This is the radical pursuit of God, the very thing we were created for and the highest call issued to mankind by our Creator. Anything less than this is adulterous and unworthy of Him.

QUESTIONS

1. Explain how our pursuit of God should resemble His pursuit of us. Why does the pursuit of self keep us from the pursuit of God? What do you need to change to pursue Christ radically?

2. How does repentance play into our pursuit of God? Is conviction the result of an angry or loving God? How do you most often respond to His conviction in your life?

3. The Lord spoke through Hosea saying, *"Their deeds do not permit them to return to their God. A spirit of prostitution is in their heart; they do not acknowledge the LORD"* (Hosea 5:4). How can our beliefs and lifestyles keep us from returning to the Lord?

4. What is spiritual prostitution? What does it look like in the church today? How do we overcome this desire to wander from the Lord?

CHAPTER THIRTEEN

Radical
DISCIPLESHIP

The Radical Jesus did not come into the world to make tame converts, but radical disciples. If He had not accomplished this task, Christianity would have ceased to exist by the end of the first century. None of those first disciples would have suffered and died for their faith had they not been thoroughly convinced that Jesus was exactly who He claimed to be. Those early believers were radicals because that is what Jesus demonstrated with His life, imparted to them through His teaching and empowered them to live through His grace.

Jesus gained disciples in many ways. Some came through His preaching; others were attracted by His miracles; and a few He personally called out. *"Follow Me"* was a command Jesus often spoke. Maybe it is the difference of culture or language, but it seems that those simple men understood what He meant when He said *"Follow Me."* When Jesus commanded them to follow, they knew it meant leaving everything to serve Him.

Jesus set the standard for true discipleship when He declared, *"If anyone comes to me and does not hate his father and mother, his wife and children, his brothers and sisters—yes, even his own life—he cannot be my disciple. Anyone who does not carry his cross and follow me cannot be my disciple"* (Luke 14:26-27). Jesus said exactly what He meant. He offered no soft path in this spiritual journey. To be His disciple meant to follow Him no matter the cost. Much of the American church has redefined discipleship to mean that we will follow Jesus if it is convenient, profitable or comfortable.

In John chapter six, Jesus described discipleship in a new and extraordinary way. He told His followers that He was the Bread of Life and that they must eat His body and drink His blood (John 6:53-55). The radical idea Jesus was presenting is that His followers must devour Him and be consumed by Him. According to Jesus, there is only one kind of discipleship and it is all-consuming. This teaching was so radical many disciples forsook Him.

However, the Master never caved in to the pressures of public opinion. His radical agenda was to bring salvation to mankind through the simple men and women who He revolutionized through His teachings. What Jesus offered was not for sale. If anything, His was the offer of the prophet: "*Come, all you who are thirsty, come to the waters; and you who have no money, come, buy and eat! Come, buy wine and milk without money and without cost*" (Isaiah 55:1). He was no huckster, trying to lure in followers with cheap promises of earthly prominence. In fact, He soundly rebuked James and John for seeking the most important positions in His kingdom (Mark 10).

The church has sunk to the despicably low spiritual condition of our day when discipleship is presented as if any halfhearted follower can partake of it. The reason for this belief is painfully simple: the church has forsaken Jesus and the truth He first delivered to the saints. The false gospel of easy-believism, which is permeating every strata of the modern church, has supplanted the true Gospel of Jesus Christ. In this false gospel, grace has become a license to sin and discipleship carries little cost or responsibility. This is a religion where people live as if heaven and hell are just different suburbs of the same kingdom. The spirit that has driven the message of easy believism is the very spirit that permeates our pagan culture.

Today, churches are full of people who do not want to live Christ's radical standards of life. They have redefined the Lord's terms of discipleship to fit their own selfish desires. Tragically, they have only deceived themselves. God will not alter His standard of faith and practice for anyone, be it popes, priests, mega-church pastors, television evangelists or the ever-elusive "good people" of the local church.

JESUS OUR EXAMPLE

One of the primary reasons for Christ's earthly ministry was to reproduce Himself in others. Jesus labored to replicate His radical nature in deformed and twisted people so He might bring them closer to God's original intent for mankind. As Christ is formed in them, the Lord commands them to reproduce His radical character in others. This is the Savior's model for Christian discipleship—radicals reproducing radicals.

Jesus not only defined the terms of discipleship but made Himself the perfect model by which all believers are to live. Once He testified, *"My food is to do the will of him who sent me and to finish his work"* (John 4:34). Later He declared, *"For I have come down from heaven not to do my will but to do the will of him who sent me"* (John 6:38). This is the essential substance of true discipleship. Jesus had His eyes and ears fixed upon the Father so He could do everything the Father commanded. In like manner, believers are to have their hearts, minds, eyes and ears fixed upon Christ so that they might become more like Him.

Love is at the center of true discipleship. Jesus stated that the *"world must learn that I love the Father and that I do exactly what my Father has commanded me"* (John 14:31). Jesus perfectly loved the Father and proved that love by obeying the Father in every way. This also demonstrates that discipleship is relational. The quality of our discipleship will be determined by the depth of our relationship with Christ. A sure sign that someone loves Him is that they are striving to be like Him in every way possible. Those who do not love Him will end up redefining discipleship according to their own selfish desires.

In another place Jesus stated, *"By myself I can do nothing; I judge only as I hear, and my judgment is just, for I seek not to please myself but him who sent me"* (John 5:30). Jesus never operated through self-rule. Those who wish to direct their own lives apart from Christ cannot be His disciples.

SPIRITUAL REPRODUCTION

One of the spiritual realities of life is that people tend to reproduce themselves, their relationship with Christ determining the quality of fruit that will come from their lives. One tell-tale sign about the lives of Christians is what can be seen in their children. On-fire believers have the greatest hope of raising up children that genuinely know Christ. Lukewarm, worldly parents can only reproduce what they themselves live.

The same dynamic can be seen in the local church. A pastor who is on-fire will typically have a group of parishioners with the same passion for God. Likewise, a carnal pastor will only be able to produce carnal disciples. Of course, such people are not Christ's disciples at all. They are disciples of a counterfeit religion, acolytes of a false god who seemingly demands little in this life, but will most certainly demand everything in the next.

True radicals for Christ reproduce their Christlikeness in others. Their passionate love for God will be contagious, their hunger for the Word infectious and their evangelism effective. Radical believers make radical disciples who form radical churches. Such people will always cause hell to tremble.

One need only look at church history to see wonderful examples of radical disciples that strove with all their being to be like Jesus, even to the laying down of their lives. These saints changed for the better both this world and eternity. Their Christlike lives brought many to saving faith. This is New Testament Christianity, the faith that Jesus birthed, the faith He calls us to love, live, advance and defend.

China is gathering an army like the world has probably never seen. In fact, it has already begun a massive invasion into Muslim, Buddhist and Hindu nations lying between China and Israel. This invasion is not military but spiritual, and it's happening because radical believers are replicating themselves.

For several decades the Chinese underground church has suffered horrendous persecutions under the Communists, yet many thousands are saved each week. These saints, many of which were martyred or spent countless years in prison, reproduced themselves in the current generation. What is this new generation doing? They have revived an old vision called "Back to Jerusalem"; they are escaping China to preach Jesus in the countries between them and Jerusalem where millions are perishing. Like their spiritual mothers and fathers, they are sacrificing themselves so others will live.

In the end, the moral and spiritual condition of children will reflect that of their parents, churches will resemble their pastors, a city will bear a likeness to the spiritual quality of its churches and a nation cannot rise any higher than the caliber of its believers. If we do not like what we see in our children, church, city or nation then there is only one honest option for us to take—to look in the mirror and give an account of ourselves to God. Until we are willing to have a personal, spiritual revolution, we cannot expect anything else to change around us for the good. Only radical disciples will bring about radical change in a family, church or nation.

Spiritual reproduction is an unalterable fact. If radical Christians reproduce themselves in others then the next generation of believers will be Christlike radicals as well. Jesus intended this to be the model of true faith throughout all generations until His second coming. But what are the ramifications if Christ's standard for discipleship is abandoned or watered down? It is the ruin of the church, which will cost multitudes their eternal soul.

QUESTIONS

1. Jesus is our example of true discipleship. How did He practice discipleship to the Father? Give some proof texts for your answer.

2. Comment on the statement, "Where Christ has the will to command, his disciples must have the will to obey." What does this have to do with discipleship?

3. What are you reproducing in others through your life and character? Look beyond the here-and-now to what your life and character will produce in your children when they are in their teens, twenties or fifties. What are you reproducing in those you work with? How about in your church family?

4. According to Jesus, discipleship is all-consuming. Why do people not want to live Christ's radical standard of discipleship? Why do people redefine the terms of discipleship to fit their own selfish desires?

CHAPTER FOURTEEN

Epilogue

Radical Christianity is about people who are being transformed into a reflection of Christ. Such people propagate Christ's spiritual and moral revolution that can turn the world upside down.

Unfortunately, most of the time our definition of radical Christianity comes from our own deformed perspectives. For instance, there are pastors who are considered radical because they have fit themselves comfortably into the pagan culture in which we live. One such pastor claimed he was radical because he tattooed his body and painted his Harley Davidson motorcycle with the skull and crossbones motif. Beer guzzling "pastors" believe themselves radical because they fearlessly step outside the "ancient paths" to adopt the customs of the world. Such nonsense is not radical by Christ's standard of radical.

Youth pastors are commonly touted as being radicals because they encourage the young people in their charge to watch carnal movies or listen to worldly music. If employing such compromising methods produces a large youth group, they are praised for their success. Youth groups are often labeled as being radical simply because they are involved in practices such as dancing, jumping and worshiping to contemporary music—none of which provides proof of a radical believer. Youth camps, Christian concerts or short-term mission trips are not reliable indicators of radical disciples either. To be radical is something far deeper.

Missionaries are often called radical because they minister in foreign lands. Of course, this is often true. History provides many accounts of missionaries who lived out the radical faith by giving their lives away overseas. However, simply because someone's field of ministry is in another country does not necessarily make them radical in the eyes of Jesus. Some are addicted to pornography; others live in wealth next to the poor they are commissioned to reach. Still others disgrace the name of Christ by being contentious with local missionaries from other denominations. Obviously, these lives are not conformed after The Radical Jesus.

Some churches are occasionally labeled as radical. This is often the case simply because they do bizarre things during worship services. Acting weird does not make one radical by God's standard. An authentic moving of the Holy Spirit is not about making people act strange but about empowering believers to rescue a world that is hell-bent towards destruction. Being radical is not about experiences, tattoos and body piercing, dancing and spinning during worship, personal prophesies or the host of other ways carnal Christians often define radical.

So what really makes a radical Christian? One thing and one thing only—Christlikeness! The more one resembles Jesus the more radical he will be. Jesus came as the Great I Am to shake nations and to emancipate mankind from sin.

Richard Wurmbrand, imprisoned for fourteen years in Communist Romania, related an account of one Christ-like pastor he met in prison. This man of God, locked away in a facility for dying prisoners, sacrificially served those around him and constantly spoke to them about Christ. One day a young man said to him, "You have told us many things about Jesus, but I still wonder what He was like to know as a man."

The pastor replied in simplicity and humility, "Jesus is like me." The young prisoner, who had frequently received compassion from this pastor, answered, "If Jesus was like you, then I love Him."

We need to be like Jesus in holiness, love, sacrifice, humility, obedience and surrender. We need to be like The Radical Jesus who was bold yet meek, fiery yet lowly, zealous yet compassionate. He is what defines normal for the human race. To be like Him means that unbelievers and worldly Christians alike will consider us extreme.

Our high calling is to be like Jesus. One glimpse of Christ's sun-radiant face and of His holy, fire-filled eyes will convince us that He is beyond radical. How will we react when we see Jesus as He is (1 John 3:2), seated upon His eternal throne? Certainly, we will be ashamed of all the excuses we have made for our cowardly, halfhearted devotion. Only in this life has the Savior offered us the phenomenal opportunity to amend our hearts and lives (Jeremiah 26:13, 35:15). Please do not foolishly squander this gift.

We must ask ourselves what can we return unto The Radical Jesus for all He has done for us (Psalms 116:12-14)? He deserves the reward of His suffering — radical, Christlike lives that bring Him glory. This is why Jesus shed His blood on Calvary. Do not give Him anything less. It is time for true believers to be like The Radical Jesus.

ABOUT THE AUTHOR

Glenn and Jessica Meldrum are the founders of In His Presence Ministries. Radically saved in the Jesus Movement from lifestyles of rebellion and drugs, they now proclaim the radical, uncompromised teachings of Jesus.

Ministry Experience

Glenn holds an M.A. in Theology and Church History from Ashland Theological Seminary and is ordained. He has ministered as an evangelist since 1997 and authored three books. His 16 years of pastoral experience has included an urban, multicultural church, a rural church and a Romanian congregation. Jessica teaches women's groups and is speaker for the Christian Women's Clubs.

The Meldrums are available for church services, evangelistic meetings and conferences providing a special emphasis in holiness, prayer and evangelism.

OTHER RESOURCES

The Radical Truth Podcast

The purpose of *The Radical Truth* podcast is simple: we want to search out the radical nature of the truth as revealed in God's Word, the Bible, and learn about Jesus our wonderful, loving Savior. We also want to learn how to live out this radical faith that Jesus created.

Rend the Heavens

Rend the Heavens was written to stir spiritually hungry saints to the dire need for a revival in our land. This book does not lay out plans, programs or strategies, but deals with the issues of the heart as they relate to revival. It was designed to help believers draw closer to Jesus through deep repentance and intimate fellowship, for this is where revival springs forth.

Rescue Me!

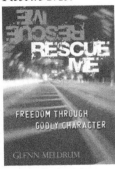

Rescue Me! is a candid investigation into how our character affects every portion of our lives. The unrefined and unconquered portions of our character are the cause for great harm. This book will help you understand how the sinful nature corrupts our character and will offer biblical answers to enable you to live the victorious life.

Floods on Dry Ground

Floods on Dry Ground is the extraordinary account of the 1949 Hebrides Awakening, when God stepped down from heaven and the things of earth took second place. For a season, God pulled back the veil separating heaven and earth in response to the prayers of desperate saints. Their prayer? "Lord forgive our waywardness and iniquities; pour water on the thirsty and floods on dry ground."

Find out more at: www.ihpministry.com or 651-247-3979:

OTHER BOOKS FROM PURE LIFE MINISTRIES

The Walk of Repentace

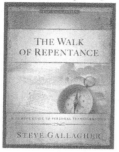

This 24-week Bible study has impacted the lives of thousands of people because it equips them to live out the Word of God. It is a simple, straightforward discipleship tool that focuses on the basics of the Christian life. Each week of this easy-to-use curriculum has a theme, addressing the challenges of the Christian life one step at a time.

Intoxicated with Babylon

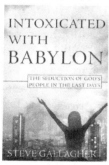

Babylon is not a place, but the seducing spirit of Antichrist. Armed with a vast array of worldly charms and enchanting indulgences, she has infiltrated pulpits and pews to deceive believers into exchanging a vibrant life in God for the empty shell of powerless religion. *Intoxicated with Babylon* is a sobering wake-up call to a slumbering and sensuous Church to return to holy living.

Walking in Truth in a World of Lies

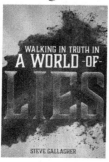

Scripture repeatedly warns of deception on a massive scale in the Last Days. So why are Christians seemingly so unconcerned? Has the abundance of Christian teaching and doctrine available today caused them to believe they are impervious to being deceived? There is only one way to stay safe from the deceiver's powerful lies: We must allow the "love of the truth" to hold sway in our innermost being.

OTHER RESOURCES AVAILABLE FROM PURE LIFE MINISTRIES

At the Altar of Sexual Idolatry
At the Altar of Sexual Idolatry DVD Curriculum
At the Altar of Sexual Idolatry Workbook
A Biblical Guide to Counseling the Sexual Addict
Create in Me a Pure Heart
Entering His Courts
From Ashes to Beauty
He Leads Me Beside Still Waters
How America Lost Her Innocence
i: the root of sin exposed
Intoxicated with Babylon
A Lamp Unto My Feet
Living in Victory
Out of the Depths of Sexual Sin
Pressing on Toward the Heavenly Calling
Selah! The Book of Psalms in the Richest Translations
Standing Firm through the Great Apostasy
The Overcomers Series (12-DVD set)
The Time of Your Life in Light of Eternity
The Walk of Repentance
Walking in Truth in a World of Lies
When His Secret Sin Breaks Your Heart
Wisdom: Proverbs & Ecclesiastes in the Richest Translations
The Word of Their Testimony

Pure Life Ministries helps Christian men achieve lasting freedom from sexual sin. The Apostle Paul said, "Walk in the Spirit and you will not fulfill the lust of the flesh." Since 1986, Pure Life Ministries (PLM) has been discipling men into the holiness and purity of heart that comes from a Spirit-controlled life. At the root, illicit sexual behavior is sin and must be treated with spiritual remedies. Our counseling programs and teaching resources are rooted in the biblical principles that, when applied to the believer's daily life, will lead him out of bondage and into freedom in Christ.

BIBLICAL TEACHING RESOURCES

Pure Life Ministries offers a full line of books, audio CDs and DVDs specifically designed to give men the tools they need to live in sexual purity.

RESIDENTIAL CARE

The most intense and involved counseling PLM offers comes through the **Residential Program** (9 months), in Dry Ridge, Kentucky. The godly and sober atmosphere on our 45-acre campus provokes the hunger for God and deep repentance that destroys the hold of sin in men's lives.

HELP AT HOME

The **Overcomers At-Home Program** (OCAH) is available for those who cannot come to Kentucky for the Residential Program. This twelve-week counseling program features weekly counseling sessions and many of the same teachings offered in the Residential Program.

CARE FOR WIVES

Pure Life Ministries also offers help to wives of men in sexual sin through our 12-week **At-Home Program for Wives**. Our wives' counselors have suffered through the trials and storms of such a discovery and can offer a devastated wife a sympathetic ear and the biblical solutions that worked in their lives.

PURE LIFE MINISTRIES

14 School St. • Dry Ridge • KY • 41035
Office: 859.824.4444 • Orders: 888.293.8714
inform@purelifeministries.org
www.purelifeministries.org

Made in the USA
Monee, IL
21 September 2021